The Simple

Crock Pot

Cookbook for Beginners

2000+ *Days of Easy and Wholesome Slow Cooker Recipes for Every Meal, From Breakfast to Dinner and Delectable Desserts*

Jonathan Jeffers

Table of Contents

INTRODUCTION

In today's fast-paced world, cooking can often feel like just another chore. Between work, family, and countless responsibilities, the thought of preparing wholesome, home-cooked meals every day might seem impossible. But what if there was a way to turn the challenge of cooking into a stress-free, even joyful, experience? Enter the Crock Pot: the kitchen tool that has been transforming lives for decades.

This humble appliance, often underestimated, is the unsung hero of the modern kitchen. It allows you to create mouthwatering dishes with minimal effort, proving that delicious meals don't have to mean hours in the kitchen. Whether you're an experienced cook or just starting out, this cookbook will be your guide to unlocking the full potential of your Crock Pot, showing you how to prepare meals that are flavorful, nutritious, and convenient. Let's explore the world of slow cooking together, where great meals are always within reach.

The Magic of Slow Cooking: Why It Works

At the heart of the Crock Pot's success lies the simple yet powerful principle of slow cooking. Unlike traditional cooking methods that rely on high heat, slow cooking uses low, consistent temperatures over extended periods of time. This gentle approach offers a number of unique advantages:

1. Unmatched Flavor Development

Slow cooking allows flavors to fully develop and mingle. Spices and herbs infuse deeply into ingredients, while natural sugars caramelize to enhance sweet-ness. The result is food with complex, robust flavors that simply cannot be achieved with faster methods.

2. Tenderizing Tough Cuts

A Crock Pot is a miracle worker for tougher, more affordable cuts of meat. Over time, the low heat breaks down connective tissues, turning these cuts into melt-in-your-mouth delicacies. Imagine a beef roast so tender it falls apart at the touch of a fork, or chicken that practically shreds itself.

3. Set It and Forget It

One of the greatest advantages of slow cooking is its convenience. Once your ingredients are in the pot, there's no need to stir, monitor, or adjust the heat. You can go about your day, confident that your meal will be ready when you need it.

4. Preserving Nutrients

Cooking at lower temperatures helps retain more vitamins and nutrients compared to high-heat methods. This makes slow cooking not only convenient but also healthier.

Why Every Kitchen Needs a Crock Pot

If you're still wondering whether a Crock Pot deserves a spot on your countertop, consider the ways it can transform your cooking experience:

1. A Time-Saving Ally

Imagine coming home from a long day at work to the aroma of a perfectly cooked meal waiting for you. With a Crock Pot, this dream becomes a reality. Prep your ingredients in the morning, set your pot, and forget about it until dinner time.

2. Perfect for All Skill Levels

Cooking can be intimidating, especially if you're

new to the kitchen. The Crock Pot eliminates guesswork with its forgiving nature. Even the simplest recipes yield impressive results.

3. Family-Friendly Meals

From hearty stews to creamy casseroles, the Crock Pot excels at creating meals that bring people together. It's the ideal tool for feeding a hungry family or hosting a dinner party with minimal effort.

4. Adaptable for All Diets

Whether you're following a specific diet like keto, paleo, vegan, or gluten-free, the Crock Pot can accommodate your needs. You'll find that this cookbook is packed with recipes for every lifestyle, ensuring that everyone can enjoy the magic of slow cooking.

5. Sustainability in the Kitchen

A Crock Pot's energy efficiency is another reason to love it. Using less electricity than an oven or stovetop, it's an eco-friendly choice that aligns with today's efforts to reduce energy consumption.

What Makes This Cookbook Special

This cookbook is not just a collection of recipes—it's a complete guide to mastering the art of slow cooking. Whether you're looking to simplify your cooking routine, explore new flavors, or create more nutritious meals, this book is here to help. Here's what you can expect:

1. The Basics of Slow Cooking

If you're a beginner, don't worry. The first chapter covers everything you need to know about using a Crock Pot, from understanding its settings to choosing the right ingredients. You'll learn tips for layering ingredients, setting cooking times, and avoiding common mistakes.

2. Over 100 Recipes for Every Occasion

This book features a diverse range of recipes, from classic comfort foods to globally inspired dishes. Whether you're craving a hearty soup, a tender roast, or a decadent dessert, there's something here for everyone.

3. Healthy and Budget-Friendly Options

Slow cooking is perfect for creating meals that are both nutritious and economical. You'll find recipes that make the most of pantry staples, seasonal produce, and affordable cuts of meat.

4. Meal Prep Made Easy

With the help of your Crock Pot, meal prepping has never been easier. This cookbook includes tips for freezing ingredients, repurposing leftovers, and planning weekly menus that save you time and effort.

The Slow Cooking Lifestyle

Cooking with a Crock Pot is more than just a method—it's a lifestyle. It's about embracing a slower pace and enjoying the process of creating food that brings comfort and joy. Here are some of the ways the Crock Pot can enhance your life:

1. Bring People Together

Food has the power to connect us, and the Crock Pot is perfect for creating dishes that can be shared. From family dinners to potlucks, it's an ideal tool for bringing people around the table.

2. Stress-Free Holidays

Hosting a holiday meal can be stressful, but the Crock Pot makes it easier. Prepare dishes in advance and let them cook while you focus on spending time with loved ones.

3. Rediscover the Joy of Home Cooking

With the convenience of a Crock Pot, you can enjoy the benefits of home-cooked meals without the hassle. There's something deeply satisfying about sitting down to a meal you've made yourself, knowing it's both delicious and nutritious.

Your Crock Pot Adventure Starts Here

This cookbook is your gateway to a new way of cooking. It's not just about saving time or simplifying your routine—it's about discovering the joy of slow cooking and the incredible meals it can produce. Whether you're making a creamy chicken and wild rice soup on a snowy day, a spicy pulled pork for game night, or a gooey chocolate lava cake to impress your guests, the Crock Pot is your ultimate kitchen ally.

So, grab your Crock Pot, gather your ingredients, and let's get started. Your journey to effortless, flavorful, and unforgettable meals begins now.

Chapter

1

Breakfasts

Layered Comfort Breakfast Bake

Prep time: 10 minutes | Cook time: 4½ hours | Serves 8 to 10

8 cups torn or cubed (1-inch) stale bread, tough crusts removed

3½ to 4 cups shredded cheese

10 large eggs

3 cups milk

1½ teaspoons salt

½ teaspoon hot sauce

1. Coat the insert of a 5- to 7-quart crock pot with nonstick cooking spray or line it with a slow-cooker liner according to the manufacturer's directions. 2. Spread a layer of the bread into the crock pot and sprinkle with some of the cheese. Continue layering the bread and cheese until it has all been used, saving some cheese for the top. 3. Whisk together the eggs, milk, salt, and hot sauce in a large bowl. Pour the mixture over the cheese and bread and push it down to make sure the bread becomes saturated. Sprinkle the remaining cheese over the top. 4. Cover and cook on low for 4 hours, until the strata is cooked through (170ºF / 77ºC on an instant-read thermometer). Remove the lid and cook for an additional 30 minutes. 5. Serve the strata from the cooker set on warm.

Crocked Blueberry French Toast

Prep time: 30 minutes | Cook time: 3 hours | Serves 12

8 eggs

½ cup plain yogurt

⅓ cup sour cream

1 teaspoon vanilla extract

½ teaspoon ground cinnamon

1 cup 2% milk

⅓ cup maple syrup

1 (1-pound / 454-g) loaf French bread, cubed

1½ cups fresh or frozen

blueberries

12 ounces (340 g) cream cheese, cubed

Blueberry Syrup:

1 cup sugar

2 tablespoons cornstarch

1 cup cold water

¾ cup fresh or frozen blueberries, divided

1 tablespoon butter

1 tablespoon lemon juice

1. In a spacious mixing bowl, combine eggs, yogurt, sour cream, vanilla extract, and cinnamon, whisking them together until smooth. Gradually incorporate the milk and maple syrup, whisking until the mixture is well-blended. 2. Spread half of the bread cubes in a greased 5- or 6-quart slow cooker, then top with half of the blueberries, cream cheese, and the egg mixture. Layer again with the remaining bread, blueberries, cream cheese, and egg mixture. Cover and refrigerate overnight. 3. Take the dish out of the fridge 30 minutes before cooking. Cover and cook on low for 3 to 4 hours or until a knife inserted near the center comes out clean. 4. To make the syrup, combine sugar and cornstarch in a small saucepan. Add water and stir until smooth. Stir in ¼ cup of blueberries and bring to a boil. Continue cooking and stirring for about 3 minutes, until the berries burst. Remove from heat, then stir in butter, lemon juice, and the remaining blueberries. Serve warm alongside the French toast.

Mediterranean Eggs

Prep time: 10 minutes | Cook time: 5 to 6 hours | Serves 4

1 tablespoon extra-virgin olive oil

12 eggs

½ cup coconut milk

½ teaspoon dried oregano

½ teaspoon freshly ground black pepper

¼ teaspoon salt

2 cups chopped spinach

1 tomato, chopped

¼ cup chopped sweet onion

1 teaspoon minced garlic

½ cup crumbled goat cheese

1. Begin by lightly greasing the slow cooker insert with olive oil. 2. In a large bowl, whisk together the eggs, coconut milk, oregano, pepper, and salt until the mixture is fully combined. 3. Stir in the spinach, tomato, onion, and garlic, ensuring everything is evenly distributed. 4. Pour the egg mixture into the prepared crock pot insert and sprinkle the crumbled goat cheese on top. 5. Cover and cook on low for 5 to 6 hours, or until the dish is firm and set, similar to a quiche. 6. Serve while warm and enjoy.

Blueberry Fancy

Prep time: 15 minutes | Cook time: 3 to 4 hours | Serves 12

1 loaf Italian bread, cubed, divided

1 pint blueberries, divided

8 ounces (227 g) cream

cheese, cubed, divided

6 eggs

1½ cups milk

1. Start by placing half of the bread cubes into the crock pot. 2. Spread half of the blueberries evenly over the bread. 3. Top the blueberries with half of the cream cheese cubes. 4. Repeat these three layers once more. 5. In a separate bowl, whisk the eggs and milk together, then pour the mixture over all the ingredients in the crock pot. 6. Cover the crock pot and cook on low until the dish is fully set and cooked through. 7. Serve and enjoy!

Creamy Coconut Nut Bowl

Prep time: 10 minutes | Cook time: 8 hours | Serves 6

1 tablespoon coconut oil	2 ounces (57 g) protein
1 cup coconut milk	powder
1 cup unsweetened	1 teaspoon ground
shredded coconut	cinnamon
½ cup chopped pecans	¼ teaspoon ground nutmeg
½ cup sliced almonds	½ cup blueberries, for
¼ cup granulated erythritol	garnish
1 avocado, diced	

1. Lightly grease the insert of a slower cooker with the coconut oil. 2. Place the coconut milk, shredded coconut, pecans, almonds, erythritol, avocado, protein powder, cinnamon, and nutmeg in the crock pot . 3. Cover and cook on low for 8 hours. 4. Stir the mixture to create the desired texture. 5. Serve topped with the blueberries.

Overnight Fruit-Infused Oats

Prep time: 5 minutes | Cook time: 8 hours | Serves 6

2 cups dry rolled oats	or raisins, or cranberries,
4 cups water	or a mixture of any of
1 teaspoon salt	these fruits
½ to 1 cup chopped dates,	

1. Combine all ingredients in crock pot . 2. Cover and cook on low overnight, or for 8 hours.

Polenta

Prep time: 10 minutes | Cook time:2 to 9 hours | Serves 8 to 10

4 tablespoons melted	6 cups boiling water
butter, divided	2 cups dry cornmeal
¼ teaspoon paprika	2 teaspoons salt

1. Begin by greasing the inside of the crock pot with 1 tablespoon of butter and sprinkle in paprika. Set the crock pot to the high setting. 2. Add the remaining ingredients to the crock pot in the order listed, including 1 tablespoon of butter. Stir the mixture thoroughly to combine. 3. Cover the crock pot and cook on high for 2 to 3 hours, or on low for 6 to 9 hours, stirring occasionally. 4. Once the polenta is cooked, pour it into 2 lightly greased loaf pans. Chill for 8 hours or overnight to set. 5. To serve, slice the chilled polenta into ¼-inch thick pieces. Heat 2 tablespoons of butter in a large nonstick skillet, then place the slices in the skillet and cook until golden brown. Flip the slices to brown the other side. 6. For a delicious breakfast, serve with your favorite sweetener.

Streusel Cake

Prep time: 10 minutes | Cook time: 3 to 4 hours | Serves 8 to 10

1 (16-ounce / 454-g)	¼ cup packed brown sugar
package pound cake mix,	1 tablespoon flour
prepared according to	¼ cup chopped nuts
package directions	1 teaspoon cinnamon

1. Generously grease and flour a 2-pound (907-g) coffee can or a crock pot baking insert that fits inside your crock pot. Pour the prepared cake mix into the can or baking insert. 2. In a small bowl, combine the brown sugar, flour, nuts, and cinnamon. Sprinkle this mixture evenly over the top of the cake mix. 3. Place the coffee can or baking insert into the crock pot, then cover the top with several layers of paper towels to catch any moisture. 4. Cover the crock pot and cook on high for 3 to 4 hours, or until a toothpick inserted into the center of the cake comes out clean. 5. Carefully remove the baking tin from the crock pot and let it cool for 30 minutes before slicing it into wedges and serving.

Slow-Cooked Keto Nut Crunch

Prep time: 10 minutes | Cook time: 3 to 4 hours | Serves 16

½ cup coconut oil, melted	shredded coconut
2 teaspoons pure vanilla	½ cup hazelnuts
extract	½ cup slivered almonds
1 teaspoon maple extract	¼ cup granulated erythritol
1 cup chopped pecans	½ teaspoon cinnamon
1 cup sunflower seeds	¼ teaspoon ground nutmeg
1 cup unsweetened	¼ teaspoon salt

1. Lightly grease the insert of the crock pot with 1 tablespoon of the coconut oil. 2. In a large bowl, whisk together the remaining coconut oil, vanilla, and maple extract. Add the pecans, sunflower seeds, coconut, hazelnuts, almonds, erythritol, cinnamon, nutmeg, and salt. Toss to coat the nuts and seeds. 3. Transfer the mixture to the insert. 4. Cover and cook on low for 3 to 4 hours, until the granola is crispy. 5. Transfer the granola to a baking sheet covered in parchment or foil to cool. 6. Store in a sealed container in the refrigerator for up to 2 weeks.

Crocked Fruited Oatmeal with Nuts

Prep time: 15 minutes | Cook time: 6 hours | Serves 6

3 cups water
2 cups old-fashioned oats
2 cups chopped apples
1 cup dried cranberries
1 cup fat-free milk
2 teaspoons butter, melted
1 teaspoon pumpkin pie spice
1 teaspoon ground cinnamon
6 tablespoons chopped almonds, toasted
6 tablespoons chopped pecans, toasted
Additional fat-free milk

1. Coat a 3-quart crock pot with cooking spray and add the first eight ingredients. Cover and cook on low for 6 to 8 hours, or until the liquid has been absorbed. 2. Spoon the oatmeal into bowls, then top with almonds and pecans. If you prefer, drizzle with extra milk before serving.

Cinnamon-Spiced Apple Breakfast Bowl

Prep time: 15 minutes | Cook time: 8 to 10 hours | Serves 8

10 apples, peeled and sliced
½ to 1 cup sugar
1 tablespoon ground cinnamon
¼ teaspoon ground nutmeg

1. Combine ingredients in crock pot . 2. Cover. Cook on low 8 to 10 hours.

Blueberry Apple Waffle Topping

Prep time: 10 minutes | Cook time: 3 hours | Serves 10 to 12

1 quart natural applesauce, unsweetened
2 Granny Smith apples, unpeeled, cored, and sliced
1 pint fresh or frozen blueberries
½ tablespoon ground
cinnamon
½ cup pure maple syrup
1 teaspoon almond flavoring
½ cup walnuts, chopped
Nonfat cooking spray

1. In a crock pot coated with nonfat cooking spray, mix together the applesauce, apples, and blueberries. 2. Stir in the cinnamon and maple syrup until well combined. 3. Cover the crock pot and cook on low for 3 hours, allowing

the flavors to meld. 4. Just before serving, add the almond flavoring and walnuts, stirring to incorporate.

Slow-Cooked Oatmeal Delight

Prep time: 10 minutes | Cook time: 2½ to 3 hours | Serves 4 to 6

⅓ cup oil
½ cup sugar
1 large egg, beaten
2 cups dry quick oats
1½ teaspoons baking powder
½ teaspoon salt
¾ cup milk

1. Pour the oil into the crock pot to grease bottom and sides. 2. Add remaining ingredients. Mix well. 3. Cook on low 2½ to 3 hours.

Overnight Oatmeal

Prep time: 5 minutes | Cook time: 3 to 10 hours | Serves 8

3¾ cups old-fashioned rolled oats
8 cups water
½ teaspoon salt
4 tablespoons (½ stick) unsalted butter, cut into
small pieces
2 cups milk or cream, warmed, for serving
¼ cup cinnamon sugar for serving

1. Lightly coat the insert of a 5- to 7-quart slow cooker with nonstick cooking spray or line it with a slow-cooker liner, following the manufacturer's instructions. 2. In the slow cooker, combine the oatmeal, water, and salt. Cover and cook on low for 8 to 10 hours or on high for 3 to 4 hours, until the oats are creamy. Stir in the butter before serving. Serve with warmed milk and a sprinkle of cinnamon sugar for extra flavor.

Morning Harvest Wassail

Prep time: 5 minutes | Cook time: 3 hours | Makes 4 quarts

1 (64-ounce / 1.8-kg) bottle cranberry juice
1 (32-ounce / 907-g) bottle apple juice
1 (12-ounce / 340-g) can frozen pineapple juice
concentrate
1 (12-ounce / 340-g) can frozen lemonade concentrate
3 to 4 cinnamon sticks
1 quart water (optional)

1. Combine all ingredients except water in crock pot . Add water if mixture is too sweet. 2. Cover. Cook on low 3 hours.

Mediterranean Spinach Frittata

Prep time: 10 minutes | Cook time: 5 to 6 hours | Serves 8

1 tablespoon extra-virgin olive oil	½ cup feta cheese
12 eggs	Cherry tomatoes, halved, for garnish (optional)
1 cup heavy (whipping) cream	Yogurt, for garnish (optional)
2 teaspoons minced garlic	Parsley, for garnish (optional)
2 cups chopped spinach	

1. Lightly grease the insert of the crock pot with the olive oil. 2. In a medium bowl, whisk together the eggs, heavy cream, garlic, spinach, and feta. Pour the mixture into the crock pot . 3. Cover and cook on low 5 to 6 hours. 4. Serve topped with the tomatoes, a dollop of yogurt, and parsley, if desired.

Salmon and Dill Strata

Prep time: 20 minutes | Cook time: 4½ hours | Serves 6 to 8

6 large eggs	zest
1 cup whole or low-fat milk	½ teaspoon freshly ground white pepper
1 cup sour cream (low fat is okay), plus additional for serving	6 plain or egg bagels, cut into ½-inch pieces
3 cups cooked salmon in chunks	1 (8-ounce / 227-g) package cream cheese, cut into ½-inch cubes
¼ cup chopped fresh dill	½ cup drained and chopped capers for serving
¼ cup finely chopped red onion	Lemon wedges for serving
2 teaspoons grated lemon	

1. Begin by preparing the insert of a 5- to 7-quart slow cooker with a light coat of nonstick cooking spray or use a slow-cooker liner according to the manufacturer's instructions. 2. In a large bowl, whisk together the eggs, milk, and sour cream until smooth. Gently fold in the salmon, dill, onion, lemon zest, and pepper. Add the cubed bagel pieces, ensuring they are thoroughly soaked in the egg mixture. 3. Layer half of the egg-bagel mixture into the crock pot, then scatter half of the cream cheese cubes on top. Repeat the layering process with the remaining mixture and cream cheese. Cover the crock pot and cook on low for 4 hours, or until the strata is fully set and reaches an internal temperature of 170ºF (77ºC) on an instant-read thermometer. Remove the lid and cook for an additional 30 minutes to achieve a golden top. 4. To serve, dish out the strata from the slow cooker set to warm, and offer sour cream, capers, and lemon wedges on the side for garnish.

Crocked Carrot Cake Oats

Prep time: 10 minutes | Cook time: 6 hours | Serves 8

4½ cups water	1 cup raisins
1 (20-ounce / 567-g) can crushed pineapple, undrained	2 teaspoons ground cinnamon
2 cups shredded carrots	1 teaspoon pumpkin pie spice
1 cup steel-cut oats	Brown sugar (optional)

1. In a 4-quart crock pot coated with cooking spray, combine the first seven ingredients. Cover and cook on low for 6 to 8 hours or until oats are tender and liquid is absorbed. Sprinkle with brown sugar if desired.

Provencal Goat Cheese Frittata

Prep time: 30 minutes | Cook time: 3 hours | Serves 6

½ cup water	1 teaspoon hot pepper sauce
1 tablespoon olive oil	½ teaspoon salt
1 medium Yukon Gold potato, peeled and sliced	¼ teaspoon pepper
1 small onion, thinly sliced	1 (4-ounce / 113-g) log fresh goat cheese, coarsely crumbled, divided
½ teaspoon smoked paprika	½ cup chopped soft sun-dried tomatoes (not packed in oil)
12 eggs	
1 teaspoon minced fresh thyme or ¼ teaspoon dried thyme	

1. Layer two 24-inch pieces of aluminum foil; starting with a long side, fold up foil to create a 1-inch wide strip. Shape strip into a coil to make a rack for bottom of a 6-quart oval crock pot . Add water to crock pot ; set foil rack in water. 2. In a large skillet, heat oil over medium-high heat. Add potato and onion; cook and stir 5 to 7 minutes or until potato is lightly browned. Stir in paprika. Transfer to a greased 1½-quart baking dish (dish must fit in crock pot). 3. In a large bowl, whisk eggs, thyme, pepper sauce, salt and pepper; stir in 2 ounces (57 g) cheese. Pour over potato mixture. Top with tomatoes and remaining goat cheese. Place dish on foil rack. 4. Cook, covered, on low 3 hours or until eggs are set and a knife inserted near the center comes out clean.

Pumpkin-Nutmeg Pudding

Prep time: 15 minutes | Cook time: 6 to 7 hours | Serves 8

¼ cup melted butter, divided
2½ cups canned pumpkin purée
2 cups coconut milk
4 eggs
1 tablespoon pure vanilla extract
1 cup almond flour

½ cup granulated erythritol
2 ounces (57 g) protein powder
1 teaspoon baking powder
1 teaspoon ground cinnamon
¼ teaspoon ground nutmeg
Pinch ground cloves

1. Begin by greasing the insert of the crock pot with 1 tablespoon of butter. 2. In a large mixing bowl, whisk together the remaining butter, pumpkin, coconut milk, eggs, and vanilla extract until fully blended. 3. In a separate small bowl, combine the almond flour, erythritol, protein powder, baking powder, cinnamon, nutmeg, and cloves. 4. Add the dry mixture to the wet ingredients, stirring until everything is well incorporated. 5. Pour the batter into the prepared crock pot insert. 6. Cover and cook on low for 6 to 7 hours, allowing the flavors to meld and the texture to set. 7. Serve warm, and enjoy!

Enchiladas Verde

Prep time: 20 minutes | Cook time: 4 to 5 hours | Serves 6 to 8

2 tablespoons vegetable oil
1 medium onion, finely chopped
1 Anaheim chile pepper, seeded and finely chopped
4 tablespoons finely chopped fresh cilantro
3 cups tomatillo salsa
½ cup chicken broth
2½ cups finely shredded

mild Cheddar cheese
2 cups finely shredded Monterey Jack or Pepper Jack cheese
2 cups crumbled queso fresco
2 cups sour cream
12 (6-inch) round white or yellow corn tortillas, cut in strips or roughly torn

1. Coat the insert of a 5- to 7-quart crock pot with nonstick cooking spray or line it with a slow-cooker liner, following the manufacturer's instructions. 2. In a medium saucepan, heat the oil over medium-high heat. Add the onion and chile, sautéing them for 3 to 5 minutes until softened and fragrant. 3. Stir in 2 tablespoons of cilantro, the salsa, and broth, then let the mixture simmer for about 30 minutes, allowing the sauce to reduce and thicken slightly. Remove from heat and set aside to cool slightly. In a separate bowl, combine the Cheddar and Monterey Jack cheese. 4. In another bowl, mix the queso fresco, remaining 2 tablespoons of cilantro, and sour cream. Stir well to combine. 5. Begin layering by spreading a thin layer of the sauce on the bottom of the crock pot insert. Add one-third of the tortillas, covering the bottom evenly. Spread half of the queso fresco mixture over the tortillas, followed by one-third of the shredded cheese. Repeat the layering with tortillas, sauce, queso fresco mixture, and shredded cheese. Finish with the remaining tortillas, sauce, and shredded cheese. Cover and cook on low for 3 to 4 hours, or until the casserole is heated through and the cheese is bubbling. Remove the cover and cook for an additional 30 to 45 minutes. 6. Serve directly from the crock pot set to warm.

Garden Fresh Veggie Omelet

Prep time: 15 minutes | Cook time: 4 to 5 hours | Serves 8

1 tablespoon extra-virgin olive oil
10 eggs
½ cup heavy (whipping) cream
1 teaspoon minced garlic
¼ teaspoon salt
⅛ teaspoon freshly ground black pepper

½ cup chopped cauliflower
½ cup chopped broccoli
1 red bell pepper, chopped
1 scallion, white and green parts, chopped
4 ounces (113 g) goat cheese, crumbled
2 tablespoons chopped parsley, for garnish

1. Lightly grease the insert of the crock pot with the olive oil. 2. In a medium bowl, whisk together the eggs, heavy cream, garlic, salt, and pepper. Stir in the cauliflower, broccoli, red bell pepper, and scallion. Pour the mixture into the crock pot . Sprinkle the top with goat cheese. 3. Cover and cook on low for 4 to 5 hours. 4. Serve topped with the parsley.

Warm Sunrise Fruit Medley

Prep time: 5 minutes | Cook time: 2 to 7 hours | Serves 8 to 9

1 (12-ounce / 340-g) package dried apricots
1 (12-ounce / 340-g) package pitted dried plums
1 (11-ounce / 312-g) can mandarin oranges in light

syrup, undrained
1 (29-ounce / 822-g) can sliced peaches in light syrup, undrained
¼ cup white raisins
10 maraschino cherries

1. Combine all ingredients in crock pot . Mix well. 2. Cover. Cook on low 6 to 7 hours, or on high 2 to 3 hours.

Southwest Sausage Hash-Brown Bake

Prep time: 25 minutes | Cook time: 2½ to 3 hours | Serves 8

1½ pounds (680 g) bulk pork sausage

2 medium onions, finely chopped

1 Anaheim chile, cored, seeded and finely chopped

1 medium red bell pepper, seeded and finely chopped

1 teaspoon ground cumin

½ teaspoon dried oregano

1 (16-ounce / 454-g) package frozen shredded hash brown potatoes,

defrosted, or 2 cups fresh shredded hash browns

6 large eggs, beaten

1 cup milk

1 cup mayonnaise

1 cup prepared salsa (your choice of heat)

2 cups shredded mild Cheddar cheese, or 1 cup shredded mild Cheddar mixed with 1 cup shredded Pepper Jack cheese

1. Coat the insert of a 5- to 7-quart crock pot with nonstick cooking spray or line the insert with a slow-cooker liner according the manufacturer's directions. 2. Cook the sausage in a large skillet over high heat until it is no longer pink, breaking up any large pieces with the side of a spoon. 3. Remove all but 1 tablespoon of fat from the pan and heat over medium-high heat. Add the onions, chile, bell pepper, cumin, and oregano and sauté until the onions are softened and translucent, 5 to 6 minutes. Transfer the mixture to a bowl and allow to cool. 4. Add the potatoes to the bowl and stir to blend. In a smaller bowl, whisk together the eggs, milk, and mayonnaise. Pour over the sausage and potato mixture and stir to combine. 5. Transfer half the mixture to the slow-cooker insert, then cover with half the salsa and half the cheese. Repeat the layers with the remaining ingredients. Cover and cook on high for 2½ to 3 hours, until the casserole is puffed, and cooked through (170ºF / 77ºC on an instant-read thermometer). Remove the cover and allow the frittata to rest for 30 minutes. 6. Serve from the cooker set on warm.

Overnight Steel-Cut Oats

Prep time: 5 minutes | Cook time: 8 hours | Serves 4 to 5

1 cup dry steel-cut oats

4 cups water

1. Add all the ingredients to the crock pot and stir to combine. 2. Cover and cook on low for 8 hours, or overnight. 3. Stir well before serving and top with your favorite toppings.

Huevos Rancheros

Prep time: 10 minutes | Cook time: 3 hours | Serves 8

1 tablespoon extra-virgin olive oil

10 eggs

1 cup heavy (whipping) cream

1 cup shredded Monterey Jack cheese, divided

1 cup prepared or homemade salsa

1 scallion, green and white parts, chopped

1 jalapeño pepper, chopped

½ teaspoon chili powder

½ teaspoon salt

1 avocado, chopped, for garnish

1 tablespoon chopped cilantro, for garnish

1. Begin by greasing the crock pot insert lightly with olive oil. 2. In a large bowl, whisk together the eggs, heavy cream, ½ cup of cheese, salsa, scallions, jalapeño, chili powder, and salt until well combined. Pour the mixture into the crock pot insert and top with the remaining ½ cup of cheese. 3. Cover the crock pot and cook on low for about 3 hours, or until the eggs are fully set and firm. 4. Allow the eggs to cool slightly before slicing into wedges. Serve with sliced avocado and a sprinkle of fresh cilantro for garnish.

Spiced Zucchini-Carrot Loaf

Prep time: 15 minutes | Cook time: 3 to 5 hours | Makes 8 slices

2 teaspoons butter, for greasing pan

1 cup almond flour

1 cup granulated erythritol

½ cup coconut flour

1½ teaspoons baking powder

1 teaspoon ground cinnamon

½ teaspoon ground nutmeg

½ teaspoon baking soda

¼ teaspoon salt

4 eggs

½ cup butter, melted

1 tablespoon pure vanilla extract

1½ cups finely grated zucchini

½ cup finely grated carrot

1. Lightly grease a 9-by-5-inch loaf pan with the butter and set aside. 2. Place a small rack in the bottom of your crock pot . 3. In a large bowl, stir together the almond flour, erythritol, coconut flour, baking powder, cinnamon, nutmeg, baking soda, and salt until well mixed. 4. In a separate medium bowl, whisk together the eggs, melted butter, and vanilla until well blended. 5. Add the wet ingredients to dry ingredients and stir to combine. 6. Stir in the zucchini and carrot. 7. Spoon the batter into the prepared loaf pan. 8. Place the loaf pan on the rack in the bottom of the crock pot , cover, and cook on high for 3 hours. 9. Remove the loaf pan, let the bread cool completely, and serve.

Summer Squash and Mushroom Strata

Prep time: 20 minutes | Cook time: 6 hours | Serves 2

1 onion, chopped
2 garlic cloves, minced
1½ cups sliced cremini mushrooms
1 red bell pepper, chopped
1 yellow summer squash, chopped
Nonstick cooking spray
6 slices French bread, cubed
1 cup shredded Cheddar cheese
1 cup shredded Swiss cheese
5 eggs, beaten
1 cup milk
1 tablespoon Dijon mustard
½ teaspoon salt
½ teaspoon dried basil leaves
⅛ teaspoon freshly ground black pepper

1. In a medium bowl, combine the onion, garlic, mushrooms, bell pepper, and squash, stirring to mix evenly. 2. Lightly spray the crock pot insert with nonstick cooking spray. 3. Layer the bread, vegetable mixture, and both Cheddar and Swiss cheeses in the crock pot. 4. In a separate bowl, whisk together the eggs, milk, mustard, salt, basil, and pepper until well combined. 5. Pour the egg mixture evenly over the layers in the crock pot. 6. Cover and cook on low for 6 hours, or until the internal temperature reaches 160ºF (71ºC) as measured with a food thermometer. 7. Once cooked, cut the casserole into squares and serve.

Egg and Broccoli Casserole

Prep time: 15 minutes | Cook time: 2½ to 3 hours | Serves 6

1 (24-ounce / 680-g) carton small-curd cottage cheese
1 (10-ounce / 283-g) package frozen chopped broccoli, thawed and drained
2 cups shredded Cheddar cheese
6 eggs, beaten
⅓ cup flour
¼ cup butter, melted
3 tablespoons finely chopped onion
½ teaspoon salt
Shredded cheese (optional)

1. In a bowl, combine the first 8 ingredients. Pour the mixture into a greased crock pot. 2. Cover and cook on high for 1 hour. Stir well, then reduce the heat to low. Cover and cook for an additional 2½ to 3 hours, or until the internal temperature reaches 160ºF (71ºC) and the eggs are set. 3. Sprinkle with cheese and serve.

Golden Maple Nut Granola

Prep time: 20 minutes | Cook time: 2 hours | Makes 5 to 6 cups

¾ cup extra-virgin olive oil, plus more for crock pot
4 cups old-fashioned rolled oats
1 cup raw shelled pistachios, almonds, walnuts, pecans, or hazelnuts, chopped if large
¼ cup packed brown sugar
½ teaspoon ground cinnamon
½ teaspoon coarse salt
½ cup pure maple syrup
1 tablespoon vanilla extract
½ cup dried apricots, dates, cherries, figs, raisins, blueberries, or cranberries, chopped if large

1. Brush the insert of a 5- to 6-quart crock pot with oil and preheat cooker. 2. Stir together oats, nuts, brown sugar, cinnamon, and ¼ teaspoon salt in the crock pot until well combined. Stir in oil, maple syrup, and vanilla, mixing until fully combined. Raise heat to high, partially cover, turning lid 45 degrees to allow moisture to escape, and cook on high, stirring every 30 minutes, until toasted and golden brown, about 2 hours (do not cook on low). After 1 hour, rotate cooker insert to prevent scorching. 3. Stir in dried fruit; then spread granola in a single layer on a rimmed baking sheet to cool completely. Sprinkle with remaining ¼ teaspoon salt, if desired. (Store in an airtight container at room temperature for up to 1 week.)

Toasted Walnut Oatmeal Delight

Prep time: 10 minutes | Cook time: 7 hours | Makes 7 cups

1 cup chopped walnuts
Nonstick cooking spray
2 cups rolled oats (not instant or quick cooking)
1 cup raisins
3 cups almond milk
1½ cups apple juice
⅓ cup honey
⅓ cup brown sugar
½ teaspoon ground cinnamon
¼ teaspoon ground nutmeg
¼ teaspoon salt

1. In a small saucepan over medium-low heat, toast the walnuts until fragrant, about 2 minutes, stirring frequently. 2. Spray the crock pot with the nonstick cooking spray. 3. In the crock pot , combine the walnuts, oats, and raisins. 4. In a large bowl, beat the almond milk, apple juice, honey, brown sugar, cinnamon, nutmeg, and salt. Pour the mixture into the crock pot . 5. Cover and cook on low for 7 hours, or until the oatmeal is thickened and tender, and serve.

Decadent Chocolate-Cherry French Toast Bake

Prep time: 15 minutes | Cook time: 6 hours | Serves 2

Nonstick cooking spray	cherries
8 slices French bread	5 eggs, beaten
¾ cup mascarpone cheese	1 cup milk
½ cup cherry preserves	1 teaspoon vanilla
¾ cup semisweet chocolate chips, melted	½ teaspoon ground cinnamon
1 cup sliced pitted fresh	¼ teaspoon salt

1. Line the crock pot with heavy-duty foil, and spray with the nonstick cooking spray. 2. Spread one side of each slice of bread with the mascarpone cheese and the cherry preserves. Drizzle with the melted chocolate. 3. Cut the bread slices in half and layer them in the crock pot with the fresh cherries. 4. In a medium bowl, beat the eggs, milk, vanilla, cinnamon, and salt. Pour the egg mixture into the crock pot . 5. Cover and cook on low for 6 hours, or until the mixture is set and registers 160ºF (71ºC) on a food thermometer. Remove from the crock pot using the foil, slice, and serve.

Sausage Breakfast Risotto

Prep time: 20 minutes | Cook time: 7 hours | Serves 2

8 ounces (227 g) pork sausage	½ cup milk
1 onion, chopped	½ teaspoon salt
2 garlic cloves, minced	½ teaspoon dried marjoram leaves
Nonstick cooking spray	⅛ teaspoon freshly ground black pepper
1 cup sliced cremini mushrooms	⅓ cup grated Parmesan cheese
1 cup Arborio rice	1 tablespoon butter
3 cups chicken stock	

1. In a medium saucepan, cook the sausage, onion, and garlic over medium heat, stirring occasionally to break up the meat, until the sausage is browned, about 10 minutes. Drain off any excess fat. 2. Lightly spray the crock pot insert with nonstick cooking spray. 3. In the crock pot, combine the sausage mixture, mushrooms, and rice. Pour in the stock and milk, and season with salt, marjoram, and pepper. Stir to combine. 4. Cover and cook on low for 7 hours, until the rice is tender and the flavors are well combined. 5. Stir in the cheese and butter. Let the dish sit for 5 minutes to allow the cheese to melt, then serve hot.

Crocked Dulce de Leche Spread

Prep time: 5 minutes | Cook time: 2 hours | Makes 2½ cups

2 (14-ounce / 397-g) cans sweetened condensed milk	Cookies, for serving

1. Place unopened cans of milk in crock pot . Fill cooker with warm water so that it comes above the cans by 1½ to 2 inches. 2. Cover cooker. Cook on high 2 hours. 3. Cool unopened cans. 4. When opened, the contents should be thick and spreadable. Use as a filling between 2 cookies.

Banana Bread Casserole

Prep time: 15 minutes | Cook time: 6 hours | Serves 2

Nonstick cooking spray	4 eggs, beaten
6 slices banana bread, cubed	1½ cups milk
6 slices French bread, cubed	⅓ cup sugar
1 banana, sliced	2 tablespoons honey
4 slices bacon, cooked and crumbled	1 teaspoon ground cinnamon
½ cup chopped pecans	1 teaspoon vanilla
	¼ teaspoon salt

1. Lightly spray the crock pot with nonstick cooking spray. 2. In the crock pot, layer the banana bread, French bread, banana slices, bacon, and pecans. 3. In a medium bowl, whisk together the eggs, milk, sugar, honey, cinnamon, vanilla, and salt until well combined. Pour the egg mixture evenly over the layered ingredients in the crock pot. 4. Cover and cook on low for 6 hours, or until the internal temperature reaches 160ºF (71ºC). Serve hot and enjoy!

Slow-Cooked Creamy Cornmeal Porridge

Prep time: 10 minutes | Cook time: 4 to 6 hours | Serves 15 to 18

2 cups cornmeal	2 cups cold water
2 teaspoons salt	6 cups hot water

1. Combine cornmeal, salt, and cold water. 2. Stir in hot water. Pour into greased crock pot . 3. Cover. Cook on high 1 hour, then stir again and cook on low 3 to 4 hours or cook on low 5 to 6 hours, stirring once every hour during the first 2 hours. 4. Serve hot.

Breakfast Prunes

Prep time: 10 minutes | Cook time: 8 to 10 hours | Serves 6

2 cups orange juice	¼ teaspoon ground nutmeg
¼ cup orange marmalade	1 cup water
1 teaspoon ground cinnamon	1 (12-ounce / 340-g) package pitted dried prunes
¼ teaspoon ground cloves	2 thin lemon slices

1. In the crock pot, combine orange juice, marmalade, cinnamon, cloves, nutmeg, and water. 2. Stir in the prunes and lemon slices. 3. Cover the crock pot and cook on low for 8 to 10 hours, or overnight for convenience. 4. Serve warm as a breakfast dish, or serve warm or chilled as a side dish with your meal later in the day.

Peach French Toast Bake

Prep time: 15 minutes | Cook time: 6 hours | Serves 2

Nonstick cooking spray	4 eggs
½ cup brown sugar	1 cup milk
3 tablespoons butter	¼ cup granulated sugar
1 tablespoon water	½ teaspoon ground cinnamon
1 teaspoon vanilla	
8 slices French bread	¼ teaspoon salt
1½ cups peeled sliced peaches	⅔ cup chopped pecans

1. Line the crock pot with heavy-duty foil and lightly coat it with nonstick spray. 2. In a small saucepan, melt the brown sugar, butter, and water over low heat. Stir occasionally and simmer for about 5 minutes until the syrup thickens. Remove from heat and stir in the vanilla extract. 3. Layer the cubed bread and sliced peaches in the crock pot, drizzling each layer with some of the warm brown sugar syrup. 4. In a bowl, whisk together the eggs, milk, granulated sugar, cinnamon, and salt until smooth. Pour the egg mixture evenly over the bread and peaches. Top with pecans. 5. Cover the crock pot and cook on low for 6 hours, or until the internal temperature reaches 160°F (71°C) and the dish is set. 6. After cooking, carefully remove the dish from the crock pot, slice it into servings, and enjoy!

Buttery Coconut Bread

Prep time: 10 minutes | Cook time: 3 to 4 hours | Makes 8 slices

1 tablespoon butter, softened	¼ teaspoon liquid stevia
6 large eggs	1 cup almond flour
½ cup coconut oil, melted	½ cup coconut flour
1 teaspoon pure vanilla extract	1 ounce (28 g) protein powder
	1 teaspoon baking powder

1. Butter an 8-by-4-inch loaf pan to prepare it for baking. 2. In a bowl, whisk the eggs, oil, vanilla extract, and stevia until smooth and well combined. 3. In a separate bowl, blend the almond flour, coconut flour, protein powder, and baking powder until evenly mixed. 4. Gradually fold the dry ingredients into the wet ingredients, mixing until just combined. 5. Pour the batter into the greased loaf pan and place the pan onto a rack inside the crock pot. 6. Cover and cook on low for 3 to 4 hours, or until a toothpick or knife inserted into the center of the loaf comes out clean. 7. Let the bread cool in the pan for 15 minutes, then carefully remove it from the pan and transfer to a wire rack to cool completely. 8. Store the cooled bread in a sealed container in the fridge for up to 7 days.

Savory Bacon & Egg Bake

Prep time: 15 minutes | Cook time: 5 to 6 hours | Serves 8

1 tablespoon bacon fat or extra-virgin olive oil	½ sweet onion, chopped
12 eggs	2 teaspoons minced garlic
1 cup coconut milk	¼ teaspoon freshly ground black pepper
1 pound (454 g) bacon, chopped and cooked crisp	⅛ teaspoon salt
	Pinch red pepper flakes

1. Lightly grease the insert of the crock pot with the bacon fat or olive oil. 2. In a medium bowl, whisk together the eggs, coconut milk, bacon, onion, garlic, pepper, salt, and red pepper flakes. Pour the mixture into the crock pot . 3. Cover and cook on low for 5 to 6 hours. 4. Serve warm.

Chapter 2 — Stews and Soups

Hearty Homestyle Veggie-Beef Soup

Prep time: 20 minutes | Cook time: 4 to 8 hours | Serves 6 to 8

1 pound (454 g) browned ground beef, or 2 cups stewing beef
2 cups sliced carrots
1 pound (454 g) frozen green beans, thawed
1 (14½-ounce / 411-g) can corn, drained, or 1 (16-ounce / 454-g) bag frozen corn, thawed
1 (28-ounce / 794-g) can diced tomatoes
3 cups beef or vegetable broth
3 teaspoons instant beef bouillon
2 teaspoons Worcestershire sauce
1 tablespoon sugar
1 tablespoon minced onion
1 (10¾-ounce / 305-g) can cream of celery soup

1. Place meat in bottom of crock pot . 2. Add remaining ingredients except celery soup. Mix well. 3. Stir in soup. 4. Cover. Cook on low 7 to 8 hours, or on high 4 hours. 5. If using stewing meat, shred and mix through soup just before serving. 6. Serve.

Spicy Monterey Bean & Tortilla Soup

Prep time: 25 minutes | Cook time: 3 to 8 hours | Serves 8

⅓ cup vegetable oil
1 large onion, finely chopped
1 clove garlic, minced
4 Anaheim chiles, seeded and chopped
1½ teaspoons chili powder
1 (14- to 15-ounce / 397- to 425-g) can chopped tomatoes, drained
2 (14- to 15-ounce / 397- to 425-g) cans pinto beans, drained and rinsed
6 cups chicken broth
2 cups cooked chorizo sausage, crumbled
(optional)
Salt and freshly ground black pepper
2 cups broken fried tortilla strips
½ cup shredded mild Cheddar or Monterey Jack cheese
½ cup sour cream, for garnish
4 green onions, chopped, using the white and tender green parts, for garnish
½ cup finely minced fresh cilantro, for garnish

1. Heat the oil in a large skillet over medium heat. Add the onion, garlic, and chiles and sauté until the vegetables are softened, about 5 minutes. Stir in the chili powder and cook, stirring, for about 1 minute, until fragrant. 2. Transfer the contents of the skillet to the insert of a 5- to 7-quart crock pot . Add the tomatoes, beans, broth, and sausage (if using). 3. Cover the crock pot and cook the soup on high for 3 to 4 hours or on low for 7 to 8 hours. 4. Season with salt and pepper. Add the tortilla strips to the soup, cover, and let stand for 10 minutes, until the strips just begin to soften. 5. Divide the cheese among 8 bowls and ladle the soup over. 6. Garnish each serving with a dollop of sour cream, chopped green onion, and minced cilantro.

Vegetable Salmon Chowder

Prep time: 15 minutes | Cook time: 3 hours | Serves 8

1½ cups cubed potatoes
1 cup diced celery
½ cup diced onions
2 tablespoons fresh parsley, or 1 tablespoon dried parsley
½ teaspoon salt
¼ teaspoon black pepper
Water to cover
1 (16-ounce / 454-g) can pink salmon
4 cups skim milk
2 teaspoons lemon juice
2 tablespoons finely cut red bell peppers
2 tablespoons finely shredded carrots
½ cup instant potatoes

1. In the crock pot, mix together the cubed potatoes, celery, onions, parsley, salt, pepper, and enough water to cover the ingredients. 2. Set the crock pot to high and cook for 3 hours, or until the vegetables are tender, adding more water if necessary. 3. Stir in the salmon, milk, lemon juice, red bell peppers, carrots, and instant potatoes. 4. Let the mixture heat for an additional hour until everything is piping hot and well combined.

Crocked Savory Beef Stew

Prep time: 10 minutes | Cook time: 10 to 12 hours | Serves 10 to 12

2 to 3 pounds (907 g to 1.4 kg) beef stewing meat
3 carrots, thinly sliced
1 (1-pound / 454-g) package frozen green peas with onions
1 (1-pound / 454-g) package frozen green beans
1 (16-ounce / 454-g) can whole or stewed tomatoes
½ cup beef broth
½ cup white wine
½ cup brown sugar
4 tablespoons tapioca
½ cup bread crumbs
2 teaspoons salt
1 bay leaf
Pepper to taste

1. Combine all ingredients in crock pot . 2. Cover. Cook on low 10 to 12 hours. 3. Serve.

Chicken-Bacon Soup

Prep time: 15 minutes | Cook time: 8 hours | Serves 8

1 tablespoon extra-virgin olive oil	2 teaspoons minced garlic
6 cups chicken broth	1½ cups heavy (whipping) cream
3 cups cooked chicken, chopped	1 cup cream cheese
1 sweet onion, chopped	1 cup cooked chopped bacon
2 celery stalks, chopped	1 tablespoon chopped fresh parsley, for garnish
1 carrot, diced	

1. Begin by greasing the crock pot insert with olive oil to prevent sticking. 2. Add the chicken broth, chicken, chopped onion, celery, carrots, and garlic to the pot. 3. Cover the crock pot and set it to cook on low for 8 hours, allowing the flavors to meld together. 4. Once the cooking time is up, stir in the heavy cream, cream cheese, and crispy bacon to create a creamy texture. 5. Before serving, sprinkle fresh parsley on top for added color and flavor.

Veracruz-Style Fish Soup

Prep time: 30 minutes | Cook time: 5 to 6 hours | Serves 8

4 (6-inch) corn tortillas, cut into thin strips	1 (28- to 32-ounce / 794- to 907-g) can chopped tomatoes, with their juice
2 tablespoons vegetable oil	
1 medium onion, finely chopped	1 (8-ounce / 227-g) bottle clam juice
2 cloves garlic, minced	1 pound (454 g) sea bass, halibut, or red snapper fillets, cut into 1-inch chunks
1 jalapeño pepper, seeded and finely chopped	
2 medium red bell peppers, finely chopped	2 cups cooked long-grain rice
1 teaspoon ground cumin	½ cup finely chopped fresh cilantro
1 teaspoon dried oregano	
1 (12-ounce / 340-g) bottle Corona or other light Mexican beer	Salt and freshly ground black pepper

1. Start by layering the tortillas at the bottom of your 5- to 7-quart crock pot insert. 2. In a large skillet, heat oil over medium-high heat. Add the chopped onion, garlic, jalapeño, bell peppers, cumin, and oregano. Sauté for about 5 minutes until the vegetables soften and become fragrant. 3. Pour in the beer, using a spatula to scrape up any browned bits from the skillet, then transfer everything to the crock pot insert and mix with the tortillas. Add the tomatoes and clam juice, stirring to combine. 4. Cover and cook on low for 4 to 5 hours, allowing the flavors to meld together. 5. Once cooked, stir in the fish, rice, and cilantro, and continue to cook for another hour until the fish is tender and fully cooked. Season with salt and pepper to taste, then serve and enjoy!

Hearty Creamy Chicken & Kale Stew

Prep time: 20 minutes | Cook time: 6 hours | Serves 6

3 tablespoons extra-virgin olive oil, divided	2 celery stalks, diced
	1 carrot, diced
1 pound (454 g) boneless chicken thighs, diced into 1½-inch pieces	1 teaspoon dried thyme
	1 cup shredded kale
	1 cup coconut cream
½ sweet onion, chopped	Salt, for seasoning
2 teaspoons minced garlic	Freshly ground black pepper, for seasoning
2 cups chicken broth	

1. Lightly grease the insert of the crock pot with 1 tablespoon of the olive oil. 2. In a large skillet over medium-high heat, heat the remaining 2 tablespoons of the olive oil. Add the chicken and sauté until it is just cooked through, about 7 minutes. 3. Add the onion and garlic and sauté for an additional 3 minutes. 4. Transfer the chicken mixture to the insert, and stir in the broth, celery, carrot, and thyme. 5. Cover and cook on low for 6 hours. 6. Stir in the kale and coconut cream. 7. Season with salt and pepper, and serve warm.

Hearty Garden Beef Stew

Prep time: 25 minutes | Cook time: 10 to 11 hours | Serves 14 to 18

2 to 3 pounds (907 g to 1.4 kg) beef, cubed	1 large onion, chopped
	4 medium potatoes, peeled and chopped
1 (16-ounce / 454-g) package frozen green beans or mixed vegetables	1 (10¾-ounce / 305-g) can tomato soup
1 (16-ounce / 454-g) package frozen corn	1 (10¾-ounce / 305-g) can celery soup
1 (16-ounce / 454-g) package frozen peas	1 (10¾-ounce / 305-g) can mushroom soup
2 pounds (907 g) carrots, chopped	Bell pepper, chopped (optional)

1. Combine all ingredients in 2 (4-quart) crock pot s (this is a very large recipe). 2. Cover. Cook on low 10 to 11 hours.

Fruity Vegetable Beef Stew

Prep time: 25 minutes | Cook time: 5½ to 6½ hours | Serves 4

¾ pound (340 g) lean beef stewing meat, cut into ½-inch cubes

2 teaspoons canola oil

1 (14½-ounce / 411-g) can fat-free beef broth

1 (14½-ounce / 411-g) can stewed tomatoes, cut up

1½ cups peeled and cubed butternut squash

1 cup thawed, frozen corn

6 dried apricot or peach halves, quartered

½ cup chopped carrots

1 teaspoon dried oregano

¼ teaspoon salt

¼ teaspoon black pepper

2 tablespoons cornstarch

¼ cup water

2 tablespoons minced fresh parsley

1. Brown the meat in oil in a nonstick skillet over medium heat, breaking it up as it cooks. 2. Transfer the browned meat to the crock pot and add the broth, tomatoes, squash, corn, apricots, carrots, oregano, salt, and pepper. Stir to combine. 3. Cover and cook on high for 5 to 6 hours, or until the meat and vegetables are tender. 4. In a small bowl, mix the cornstarch with water until smooth. Stir the mixture into the stew. 5. Cook on high for an additional 30 minutes, or until the stew has thickened. 6. Stir in the parsley just before serving.

Hearty Pasta e Fagioli Soup

Prep time: 30 minutes | Cook time: 7½ hours | Serves 8

1 pound (454 g) ground beef

1 medium onion, chopped

1 (32-ounce / 907-g) carton chicken broth

2 (14½-ounce / 411-g) cans diced tomatoes, undrained

1 (15-ounce / 425-g) can white kidney or cannellini beans, rinsed and drained

2 medium carrots, chopped

1½ cups finely chopped

cabbage

1 celery rib, chopped

2 tablespoons minced fresh basil or 2 teaspoons dried basil

2 garlic cloves, minced

½ teaspoon salt

½ teaspoon pepper

1 cup ditalini or other small pasta

Grated Parmesan cheese (optional)

1. In a large skillet, cook beef and onion over medium heat until beef is no longer pink and onion is tender; drain. 2. Transfer to a 4- or 5-quart crock pot . Stir in the broth, tomatoes, beans, carrots, cabbage, celery, basil, garlic, salt and pepper. Cover and cook on low for 7 to 8 hours or until vegetables are tender. 3. Stir in pasta. Cover and cook on high 30 minutes longer or until pasta is tender. Sprinkle with cheese if desired.

Chicken-Nacho Soup

Prep time: 15 minutes | Cook time: 6 hours | Serves 8

3 tablespoons extra-virgin olive oil, divided

1 pound (454 g) ground chicken

1 sweet onion, diced

1 red bell pepper, chopped

2 teaspoons minced garlic

2 tablespoons taco seasoning

4 cups chicken broth

2 cups coconut milk

1 tomato, diced

1 jalapeño pepper, chopped

2 cups shredded Cheddar cheese

½ cup sour cream, for garnish

1 scallion, white and green parts, chopped, for garnish

1. Heat the olive oil in a large skillet over medium-high heat. Add diced chicken and cook until browned, about 6 minutes. 2. Remove the chicken from the skillet and set aside. In the same skillet, sauté chopped onion, bell pepper, and garlic for 3 minutes, adding taco seasoning for extra flavor. 3. Transfer the sautéed vegetables to the crock pot and stir in the cooked chicken. 4. Add coconut milk, diced tomatoes, broth, and finely chopped jalapeño for a spicy kick. 5. Cover the crock pot and cook on low for 6 hours, allowing the flavors to develop. 6. Stir in shredded cheese until fully melted, then adjust seasoning to taste. 7. Serve the dish with a dollop of sour cream and a sprinkle of fresh cilantro for extra freshness.

French Market Soup

Prep time: 10 minutes | Cook time: 10 hours | Serves 8

2 cups dry bean mix, washed with stones removed

2 quarts water

1 ham hock

1 teaspoon salt

¼ teaspoon pepper

1 (16-ounce / 454-g) can tomatoes

1 large onion, chopped

1 garlic clove, minced

1 chili pepper, chopped, or

1 teaspoon chili powder

¼ cup lemon juice

1. Add all the ingredients to the crock pot. 2. Cover and cook on low for 8 hours. Afterward, turn the heat to high and continue cooking for 2 more hours, or until the beans are tender. 3. Remove the ham bone, cut the meat into bite-sized pieces, and stir it back into the soup.

Chinese Chicken Soup

Prep time: 5 minutes | Cook time: 1 to 2 hours | Serves 6

3 (14½-ounce / 411-g) cans chicken broth

1 (16-ounce / 454-g) package frozen stir-fry vegetable blend

2 cups cooked chicken, cubed

1 teaspoon minced fresh ginger root

1 teaspoon soy sauce

1. Combine all ingredients in the crock pot, stirring to mix them well. 2. Cover and cook on high for 1 to 2 hours, adjusting the cooking time depending on whether you prefer your vegetables to be crunchy or soft.

Creamy Cheddar Broccoli Soup

Prep time: 10 minutes | Cook time: 8 to 10 hours | Serves 8

2 (16-ounce / 454-g) packages frozen chopped broccoli

2 (10¾-ounce / 305-g) cans Cheddar cheese soup

2 (12-ounce / 340-g) cans evaporated milk

¼ cup finely chopped onions

½ teaspoon seasoned salt

¼ teaspoon pepper

Sunflower seeds (optional)

Crumbled bacon (optional)

1. Combine all ingredients except sunflower seeds and bacon in crock pot . 2. Cover. Cook on low 8 to 10 hours. 3. Garnish with sunflower seeds and bacon.

Ham and Potato Chowder

Prep time: 10 minutes | Cook time: 8 hours | Serves 5

1 (5-ounce / 142-g) package scalloped potatoes

Sauce mix from potato package

1 cup cooked ham, cut into narrow strips

4 cups chicken broth

1 cup chopped celery

⅓ cup chopped onions

Salt to taste

Pepper to taste

2 cups half-and-half

⅓ cup flour

1. In the crock pot, combine diced potatoes, chopped ham, sliced celery, onions, and vegetable broth. Add the sauce mix, a pinch of salt, and pepper to season. Stir everything together. 2. Cover the crock pot and cook on low for 6 to 8 hours until the potatoes are tender. 3. In a separate bowl, whisk together flour and half-and-half until smooth, then slowly pour it into the crock pot while stirring to incorporate. 4. Continue cooking on low for an additional 30 minutes to 1 hour, stirring occasionally, until the soup thickens and becomes creamy. 5. Adjust seasoning to taste before serving, and garnish with chopped parsley or shredded cheese if desired.

Rainbow Lentil and Pea Soup

Prep time: 15 minutes | Cook time: 4 to 8 hours | Serves 8

2 tablespoons olive oil

1 large onion, chopped

4 medium carrots, diced

4 stalks celery, diced

2 teaspoons dried thyme

1 bay leaf

2 cups dried green split

peas

1 cup dried yellow split peas

½ cup dried red lentils

8 cups vegetable broth

Salt and freshly ground black pepper

1. Heat the oil in a skillet over medium-high heat. Add the onion, carrots, celery, thyme, and bay leaf and sauté until the vegetables begin to soften, 4 to 5 minutes. 2. Transfer the contents of the skillet to the insert of a 5- to 7-quart crock pot and add the split peas, lentils, and broth, and stir to combine. 3. Cover the crock pot and cook on high for 4 hours or on low for 8 hours; check the soup at 3 or 7 hours to make sure that it isn't sticking to the pot. If it appears too thick, add more broth. 4. Season with salt and pepper before serving.

Quick-to-Mix Vegetable Soup

Prep time: 5 minutes | Cook time: 5 to 7 hours | Serves 4

2 cups frozen vegetables

¾ cup fat-free, low-sodium beef gravy

1 (16-ounce / 454-g) can diced tomatoes

¼ cup dry red wine

½ cup diced onions

1 teaspoon crushed garlic

¼ teaspoon black pepper

½ cup water

1. In the crock pot, combine a mix of hearty root vegetables like potatoes, carrots, and parsnips, with diced onions, minced garlic, and a generous amount of dried herbs like thyme and oregano. Add vegetable or chicken broth, a splash of white wine, and season with salt and freshly cracked black pepper. 2. Cover and cook on high for 5 hours or on low for 7 hours, until the vegetables are tender and the flavors have fully developed. 3. For a creamier texture, stir in a dollop of heavy cream or coconut milk just before serving.

Beef Barley Stew

Prep time: 15 minutes | Cook time: 9 to 10 hours | Serves 6

½ pound (227 g) lean round steak, cut in ½-inch cubes

4 carrots, peeled and cut in ¼-inch slices

1 cup chopped yellow onions

½ cup coarsely chopped green bell peppers

1 clove garlic, pressed

½ pound (227 g) fresh button mushrooms,

quartered

¾ cup dry pearl barley

½ teaspoon salt

¼ teaspoon ground black pepper

½ teaspoon dried thyme

½ teaspoon dried sweet basil

1 bay leaf

5 cups fat-free, low-sodium beef broth

1. In the crock pot, mix together cubed root vegetables, such as sweet potatoes, carrots, and parsnips, with diced onions, garlic, and fresh herbs like thyme and rosemary. Add vegetable broth, a splash of apple cider vinegar, and season with salt and pepper to taste. 2. Cover and cook on low for 8 to 10 hours, allowing the flavors to meld together and the vegetables to become tender. 3. Serve the hearty stew as a comforting side dish, or blend it slightly for a creamy texture, adding extra broth if needed.

Back Bay Corn Chowder

Prep time: 15 minutes | Cook time: 3½ to 7½ hours | Serves 8

8 strips bacon, cut into ½-inch dice

1 cup finely chopped onion

3 stalks celery, finely chopped

1½ teaspoons dried thyme leaves

½ cup all-purpose flour

4 cups chicken or

vegetable broth

Tabasco sauce

4 cups diced red potatoes

1 (16-ounce / 454-g) package frozen petite white corn, defrosted

1 cup heavy cream

Salt

1. In a large pot, cook diced bacon over medium heat until crisp. Remove and set aside, leaving a small amount of fat in the pot. Sauté chopped onions, celery, and fresh thyme in the bacon drippings until softened and aromatic. Add flour and cook for 2-3 minutes, stirring constantly, until lightly golden. Gradually pour in your choice of chicken or vegetable broth, along with a few dashes of hot sauce, whisking to create a smooth base. Bring the mixture to a gentle simmer. 2. Transfer the sautéed ingredients into the crock pot. Add cubed potatoes, corn kernels, and any extra

seasonings like smoked paprika or a bay leaf for depth. Stir to combine. Cover and cook on high for 3 hours, or on low for 6–7 hours, until the potatoes are tender. 3. Once done, stir in a generous pour of half-and-half or full-fat cream, and continue cooking on low for an additional 30 minutes to thicken and meld the flavors. 4. Before serving, taste and adjust with more hot sauce or salt to your preference. Ladle into bowls and top with the crispy bacon crumbles for extra texture. Serve hot and enjoy!

Hearty Wild Rice and Squash Soup

Prep time: 15 minutes | Cook time: 4 to 6 hours | Serves 8

2 tablespoons butter

½ cup dry wild rice

6 cups fat-free, low-sodium chicken stock

½ cup minced onions

½ cup minced celery

½ pound (227 g) winter

squash, peeled, seeded, cut in ½-inch cubes

2 cups cooked chicken, chopped

½ cup browned, slivered almonds

1. Melt butter in small skillet. Add rice and sauté for 10 minutes over low heat. Transfer to crock pot . 2. Add all remaining ingredients except chicken and almonds. 3. Cover. Cook on low 4 to 6 hours. One hour before serving stir in chicken. 4. Top with browned slivered almonds just before serving.

Beef and Barley Paprika Stew

Prep time: 20 minutes | Cook time: 5 hours | Serves 8

2 tablespoons oil

1½ pounds (680 g) beef cubes

2 large onions, diced

1 medium green pepper, chopped

1 (28-ounce / 794-g) can whole tomatoes

½ cup ketchup

⅔ cup dry small pearl

barley

1 teaspoon salt

½ teaspoon pepper

1 tablespoon paprika

1 (10-ounce / 283-g) package frozen baby lima beans

3 cups water

1 cup sour cream

1. Brown beef cubes in oil in skillet. Add onions and green peppers. Sauté. Pour into crock pot . 2. Add remaining ingredients except sour cream. 3. Cover. Cook on high 5 hours. 4. Stir in sour cream before serving. 5. Serve.

Classic Chicken and Vegetable Dumpling Soup

Prep time: 30 minutes | Cook time: 4¼ to 6¼ hours | Serves 8

Soup:
4 cups cooked chicken, cubed
6 cups fat-free, low-sodium chicken broth
1 tablespoon fresh parsley, or 1½ teaspoons dry parsley flakes
1 cup onions, chopped
1 cup celery, chopped
6 cups diced potatoes
1 cup green beans
1 cup carrots
1 cup peas (optional)
Dumplings: (optional)
2 cups flour (half white and half whole wheat)
1 teaspoon salt
4 teaspoons baking powder
1 egg, beaten
2 tablespoons olive oil
⅔ cup skim milk

1. Combine all soup ingredients, except peas. 2. Cover. Cook on low 4 to 6 hours. 3. Transfer to large soup kettle with lid. Add peas, if desired. Bring to a boil. Reduce to simmer. 4. To make Dumplings, combine flour, salt, and baking powder in a large bowl. 5. In a separate bowl, combine egg, olive oil, and milk until smooth. Add to flour mixture.

Creamy New England Fish Chowder

Prep time: 25 minutes | Cook time: 3½ to 4 hours | Serves 8

8 strips thick-cut bacon, cut into ½-inch pieces
1 large onion, finely chopped
4 stalks celery, finely chopped
1 teaspoon dried thyme
3 tablespoons all-purpose flour
3 cups chicken broth
2 (8-ounce / 227-g) bottles clam juice
5 medium red or Yukon
gold potatoes, cut into ½-inch chunks
1 bay leaf
1½ pounds (680 g) thick-fleshed fish, such as sea bass, halibut, haddock, or cod, cut into 2-inch cubes
1½ cups heavy cream
¼ cup finely chopped fresh Italian parsley, for garnish
¼ cup finely chopped fresh chives, for garnish

1. Cook the bacon in a large skillet over medium-high heat until crisp and remove it to paper towels to drain. Remove all but ¼ cup of the bacon drippings from the skillet. 2. Add the onion, celery, and thyme and sauté until the onion is translucent, 5 to 7 minutes. Stir in the flour and cook for

3 minutes, whisking the roux constantly. Gradually stir in the broth and clam juice and bring to a boil. 3. Transfer the contents of the skillet to the insert of a 5- to 7-quart crock pot . Add the potatoes and bay leaf. Cover and cook on high for 2½ to 3 hours, until the potatoes are tender. 4. Stir in the bacon, fish, and cream. Cover and cook for an additional 45 minutes to 1 hour, until the fish is cooked through. 5. Remove the bay leaf and serve the chowder garnished with the parsley and chives.

Rustic Minestrone with Parmesan Rind

Prep time: 25 minutes | Cook time: 3 to 8 hours | Serves 8

2 tablespoons extra-virgin olive oil
3 cloves garlic, minced
1 cup coarsely chopped sweet onion
1 cup coarsely chopped carrots
1 cup coarsely chopped celery
1 tablespoon finely chopped fresh rosemary
1 (14- to 15-ounce / 397- to 425-g) can plum tomatoes, with their juice
¼ cup dry white wine
2 medium zucchini, cut into ½-inch rounds
1 (14- to 15-ounce / 397- to 425-g) can small white beans, drained and rinsed
1 head escarole or Savoy
cabbage, cut into small pieces
8 ounces (227 g) green beans, ends snipped, cut into 1-inch pieces
1 medium head cauliflower, cut into florets
Rind from Parmigiano-Reggiano cheese, cut into ½-inch pieces, plus ½ to 1 cup finely grated Parmigiano-Reggiano cheese, for garnish
2 cups vegetable broth
1 teaspoon salt
½ teaspoon freshly ground black pepper
8 ounces (227 g) cooked small pasta (shells, ditalini, or other short tubular pasta)

1. Heat the oil in a large skillet over medium-high heat. Add the garlic, onion, carrots, celery, and rosemary and sauté until the vegetables begin to soften, 4 to 5 minutes. 2. Add the tomatoes and wine and allow some of the liquid to evaporate in the pan. 3. Transfer the contents of the skillet to the insert of a 5- to 7-quart crock pot . Add the zucchini, white beans, cabbage, green beans, cauliflower, Parmigiano-Reggiano rind, broth, salt, and pepper. 4. Cover the crock pot and cook on high for 3 to 4 hours or on low for 6 to 8 hours. 5. Stir in the cooked pasta at the end of the cooking time, cover, and set on warm until ready to serve. 6. Serve the soup garnished with the grated Parmigiano-Reggiano.

Hearty Bean Soup

Prep time: 30 minutes | Cook time: 4 to 5 hours | Serves 6

3 (15-ounce / 425-g) cans pinto beans, undrained
3 (15-ounce / 425-g) cans Great Northern beans, undrained
4 cups chicken or vegetable broth
3 potatoes, peeled and chopped
4 carrots, sliced
2 celery ribs, sliced
1 large onion, chopped
1 green pepper, chopped
1 sweet red pepper, chopped (optional)
2 garlic cloves, minced
1 teaspoon salt, or to taste
¼ teaspoon pepper, or to taste
1 bay leaf (optional)
½ teaspoon liquid barbecue smoke (optional)

1. Place the beans into a 6-quart crock pot, or divide the ingredients between two smaller (4- to 5-quart) crock pots. Cover and set aside while you prep the vegetables. 2. In a separate large pot, bring the broth and vegetables to a simmer over medium heat. Cook until the vegetables are tender-crisp, about 10 minutes. Once done, transfer the cooked vegetables and broth to the crock pot. 3. Stir in the remaining ingredients, making sure everything is well combined. 4. Cover and cook on low for 4 to 5 hours, allowing the flavors to meld and the beans to soften. 5. Once ready, serve hot and enjoy the hearty, flavorful dish!

Mixed Shellfish Chowder

Prep time: 20 minutes | Cook time: 5 hours | Serves 8

4 tablespoons (½ stick) unsalted butter
1 medium onion, finely chopped
3 stalks celery, finely chopped
1 teaspoon sweet paprika
½ teaspoon dried thyme
3 tablespoons all-purpose flour
6 cups lobster stock
2 tablespoons brandy
½ pound (227 g) cooked lobster meat, picked over for shells and cartilage
½ pound (227 g) lump crab meat, picked over for shells and cartilage
¼ pound (113 g) bay or sea scallops, cut into quarters
1 cup heavy cream
¼ cup finely chopped fresh chives, for garnish

1. In a saucepan, melt the butter over medium-high heat. Add the onion, celery, paprika, and thyme, sautéing for about 3 minutes until the vegetables begin to soften. Stir in the flour and cook for 2 to 3 minutes, constantly whisking to form a smooth roux. Slowly whisk in the stock and brandy, then bring to a simmer. 2. Transfer the mixture to the insert of a 5- to 7-quart crock pot. Cover and cook on low for 4 hours, allowing the flavors to develop. 3. After 4 hours, add the lobster, crab, and scallops, then stir in the cream. Cover and cook for an additional hour on low. 4. Serve the creamy seafood soup hot, garnished with freshly chopped chives.

Hearty Tomato Beef Stew

Prep time: 15 minutes | Cook time: 8 hours | Serves 6 to 8

5 pounds (2.3 kg) stewing meat, cubed
2 onions, chopped
1 (14½-ounce / 411-g) can chopped tomatoes
1 (10¾-ounce / 305-g) can tomato soup
5 to 6 carrots, sliced
5 to 6 potatoes, peeled and cubed
1 cup sliced celery
1 bell pepper, sliced
2 teaspoons salt
½ teaspoon pepper
2 cloves minced garlic

1. Combine all ingredients in crock pot . 2. Cover. Cook on low 8 hours. 3. Serve.

Green Bean and Sausage Soup

Prep time: 25 minutes | Cook time: 7 to 10 hours | Serves 5 to 6

1 medium onion, chopped
2 carrots, sliced
2 ribs celery, sliced
1 tablespoon olive oil
5 medium potatoes, cubed
1 (10-ounce / 283-g) package frozen green beans
2 (14½-ounce / 411-g) cans chicken broth
2 broth cans water
⅓ pound (151 g) link
sausage, sliced, or bulk sausage, browned
2 tablespoons chopped fresh parsley, or 2 teaspoons dried
1 to 2 tablespoons chopped fresh oregano, or 1 to 2 teaspoons dried
1 teaspoon Italian spice
Salt to taste
Pepper to taste

1. Heat oil in a skillet over medium heat. Add the onion, carrots, and celery, sautéing until they begin to soften and develop some color, about 5 minutes. 2. Transfer the sautéed vegetables to the crock pot and add the remaining ingredients. Stir to combine. 3. Cover and cook on high for the first 1 to 2 hours to bring out the flavors, then reduce to low and cook for 6 to 8 hours until everything is tender and well-blended. 4. Taste and adjust seasoning, then serve hot as a comforting meal.

Hearty Vegetarian Kale and Bean Chili

Prep time: 10 minutes | Cook time: 4 to 9½ hours | Serves 8

1 large onion, chopped
1 tablespoon margarine
1 clove garlic, finely chopped
2 teaspoons chili powder
½ teaspoon dried oregano, crumbled
2 (14½-ounce / 411-g) cans vegetable broth
1 (14½-ounce / 411-g) can no-salt-added stewed or

diced tomatoes
5 cups water
½ teaspoon salt
¼ teaspoon black pepper
¾ pound (340 g) fresh kale
⅓ cup white long-grain rice
1 (19-ounce / 539-g) can cannellini beans, drained and rinsed

1. Sauté onion in skillet with margarine until tender. 2. Add garlic, chili powder, and oregano. Cook for 30 seconds. Pour into crock pot . 3. Add remaining ingredients except kale, rice, and beans. 4. Cover. Cook on low 7 hours, or on high 3 to 4 hours. 5. Cut kale stalks into small pieces and chop leaves coarsely. 6. Add to soup with rice and beans. 7. Cover. Cook on high 1 to 2½ hours more, or until rice is tender and kale is done to your liking.

Zesty Sausage and Beef Meatball Soup

Prep time: 25 minutes | Cook time: 6 to 8 hours | Serves 8 to 10

1 pound (454 g) ground beef
1 pound (454 g) bulk spicy sausage (casings removed)
Half a large onion, chopped
2 cups chopped carrots
2 cups chopped celery
1 green or red bell pepper, chopped (optional)
2 teaspoons salt, or to taste
¼ teaspoon pepper, or to

taste
1 teaspoon dried oregano, or to taste
2 or 3 garlic cloves, minced
1 (14½-ounce / 411-g) can stewed tomatoes with chilies
1 (14½-ounce / 411-g) can green beans
¼ teaspoon chili powder
1 cup instant rice, uncooked

1. Combine beef, sausage, and onions. Form into balls. Place in crock pot . 2. Add all remaining ingredients, except rice. Stir gently so as not to break up the meatballs. 3. Cover. Cook on low 6 to 8 hours. Stir in rice 20 minutes before serving. 4. Serve.

The Tabasco Veggie Soup

Prep time: 20 minutes | Cook time: 9 hours | Serves 8

2 (14½-ounce / 411-g) cans vegetable broth
2 vegetable bouillon cubes
4 cups water
1 quart canned tomatoes
3 to 4 garlic cloves, minced
1 large onion, chopped
1 cup chopped celery

2 cups chopped carrots
1 small zucchini, cubed
1 small yellow squash, cubed
2 teaspoons fresh basil
1 teaspoon fresh parsley
Pepper to taste
3 dashes Tabasco sauce

1. Place all the ingredients into the slow cooker. 2. Secure the lid and set the cooker to low heat, allowing it to cook for 9 hours.

Spicy Bean Soup with Cornmeal Dumplings

Prep time: 20 minutes | Cook time: 4½ to 12½ hours | Serves 4

Soup:
1 (15½-ounce / 439-g) can red kidney beans, rinsed and drained
1 (15½-ounce / 439-g) can black beans, pinto beans, or Great Northern beans, rinsed and drained
3 cups water
1 (14½-ounce / 411-g) can Mexican-style stewed tomatoes
1 (10-ounce / 283-g) package frozen whole-kernel corn, thawed
1 cup sliced carrots
1 cup chopped onions

1 (4-ounce / 113-g) can chopped green chilies
2 tablespoons instant beef, chicken, or vegetable bouillon granules
1 to 2 teaspoons chili powder
2 cloves garlic, minced
Dumplings:
⅓ cup flour
¼ cup yellow cornmeal
1 teaspoon baking powder
Dash of salt
Dash of pepper
1 egg white, beaten
2 tablespoons milk
1 tablespoon oil

1. Combine 11 soup ingredients in crock pot . 2. Cover. Cook on low 10 to 12 hours, or on high 4 to 5 hours. 3. Make dumplings by mixing together flour, cornmeal, baking powder, salt, and pepper. 4. Combine egg white, milk, and oil. Add to flour mixture. Stir with fork until just combined. 5. At the end of the soup's cooking time, turn crock pot to high. Drop dumpling mixture by rounded teaspoonfuls to make 8 mounds atop the soup. 6. Cover. Cook for 30 minutes (do not lift cover).

Taco Chicken Soup

Prep time: 10 minutes | Cook time: 5 to 7 hours | Serves 4 to 6

1 envelope dry reduced-sodium taco seasoning
1 (32-ounce / 907-g) can low-sodium V-8 juice
1 (16-ounce / 454-g) jar salsa

1 (15-ounce / 425-g) can black beans
1 cup frozen corn
1 cup frozen peas
2 whole chicken breasts, cooked and shredded

1. Add all ingredients to the crock pot, reserving the corn, peas, and chicken. 2. Cover and cook on low for 4 to 6 hours. One hour before serving, stir in the remaining vegetables and chicken.

Ham 'n Cheese Soup

Prep time: 15 minutes | Cook time: 6¼ to 8¼ hours | Serves 7

2 cups potatoes, cubed (you decide whether to peel or not)
1½ cups water
1½ cups cooked ham, cubed
1 large onion, chopped
3 tablespoons butter or

margarine
3 tablespoons flour
¼ teaspoon black pepper
3 cups fat-free milk
6 ounces (170 g) low-fat shredded cheese
1 cup frozen broccoli, thawed and chopped

1. Place all ingredients into the crock pot, leaving the cheese and broccoli aside. 2. Set the cooker to low and let it cook for 6 to 8 hours. 3. Stir in the cheese and broccoli, then cook for an additional 15 minutes or until the cheese is melted and the broccoli is heated through.

Creamy Spinach and Potato Soup

Prep time: 20 minutes | Cook time: 8 hours | Serves 2

4 cups vegetable broth
2 russet potatoes, peeled and cubed
1 onion, chopped
½ cup chopped leeks
2 garlic cloves, minced

½ teaspoon salt
½ teaspoon dried marjoram
⅛ teaspoon freshly ground black pepper
2 cups baby spinach leaves

1. In the crock pot , combine the broth, potatoes, onion, leeks, garlic, salt, marjoram, and pepper, and stir. 2. Cover and cook on low for 7½ hours. 3. Using an immersion blender or potato masher, blend or mash the ingredients so the soup is fairly smooth but still has texture. 4. Add the spinach, cover, and cook on low for another 20 to 30 minutes, or until the spinach is wilted. 5. Ladle the soup into 2 bowls and serve.

Classic Chicken Noodle Soup with Veggies

Prep time: 15 minutes | Cook time: 5 to 7 hours | Serves 6

2 onions, chopped
2 cups sliced carrots
2 cups sliced celery
1 (10-ounce / 283-g) package frozen peas (optional)
2 teaspoons salt (optional)
¼ teaspoon black pepper
½ teaspoon dried basil

¼ teaspoon dried thyme
3 tablespoons dry parsley flakes
4 cups water
2½ to 3 pounds (1.1 to 1.4 kg) chicken, cut-up
1 cup thin noodles, uncooked

1. Place all ingredients in crock pot , except chicken and noodles. 2. Remove skin and any fat from chicken pieces. Then place chicken in cooker, on top of the rest of the ingredients. 3. Cover. Cook on high 4 to 6 hours. 4. One hour before serving, remove chicken. 5. Cool slightly. Cut meat from bones. Return meat to cooker. Add noodles. 6. Cover. Cook on high 1 hour.

Jeanne's Vegetable-Beef Borscht

Prep time: 20 minutes | Cook time: 8 to 10 hours | Serves 8

1 pound (454 g) beef roast, cooked and cubed
Half a head of cabbage, sliced thinly
3 medium potatoes, diced
4 carrots, sliced
1 large onion, diced
1 cup tomatoes, diced
1 cup corn

1 cup green beans
2 cups beef broth
2 cups tomato juice
¼ teaspoon garlic powder
¼ teaspoon dill seed
2 teaspoons salt
½ teaspoon pepper
Water
Sour cream

1. Combine all the ingredients, excluding the water and sour cream. Add enough water to fill the crock pot about three-quarters full. 2. Cover and cook on low for 8 to 10 hours. 3. Serve each portion with a dollop of sour cream on top.

Simple Texas Chili

Prep time: 20 minutes | Cook time: 7 to 8 hours | Serves 4

¼ cup extra-virgin olive oil
1½ pounds (680 g) beef sirloin, cut into 1-inch chunks
1 sweet onion, chopped
2 green bell peppers, chopped
1 jalapeño pepper, seeded, finely chopped
2 teaspoons minced garlic
1 (28-ounce / 794-g) can diced tomatoes
1 cup beef broth
3 tablespoons chili powder
½ teaspoon ground cumin
¼ teaspoon ground coriander
1 cup sour cream, for garnish
1 avocado, diced, for garnish
1 tablespoon cilantro, chopped, for garnish

1. Coat the crock pot insert with 1 tablespoon of olive oil. 2. Heat the remaining 2 tablespoons of olive oil in a large skillet over medium-high heat. Add the beef and cook, breaking it up as it browns, for about 8 minutes. 3. Stir in the onion, bell peppers, jalapeño, and garlic, cooking for another 4 minutes until softened. 4. Transfer the beef and veggie mix to the crock pot, then add in the tomatoes, broth, chili powder, cumin, and coriander, stirring to combine. 5. Cover and let it cook on low for 7 to 8 hours, allowing the flavors to meld. 6. Serve the dish topped with sour cream, fresh avocado, and a sprinkle of cilantro.

Taco Soup Plus

Prep time: 15 minutes | Cook time: 6 to 8 hours | Serves 6

Soup:
1 pound (454 g) extra-lean ground beef or ground turkey
1 medium onion, chopped
1 medium green bell pepper, chopped
1 envelope dry reduced-sodium taco seasoning
½ cup water
4 cups reduced-sodium vegetable juice
1 cup chunky salsa
Toppings:
¾ cup shredded lettuce
6 tablespoons fresh tomato, chopped
6 tablespoons reduced-fat Cheddar cheese, shredded
¼ cup green onions or chives, chopped
¼ cup fat-free sour cream or fat-free plain yogurt
Baked tortilla or corn chips

1. Brown the meat and onion together in a nonstick skillet, then drain any excess fat. 2. Add all the soup ingredients to the crock pot and stir to combine. 3. Cover and cook on low for 6 to 8 hours, allowing the flavors to develop. 4. Serve

the soup with your favorite toppings.

Creamy Clam Chowder

Prep time: 15 minutes | Cook time: 2½ hours | Serves 8

2 (1-pound / 454-g) cans low-fat, low-sodium chicken broth
3 large potatoes, peeled and diced finely
2 large onions, chopped finely
1 (1-pound / 454-g) can creamed corn
1 carrot, chopped finely
1 dozen littleneck clams,
or 3 (6-ounce / 170-g) cans minced clams
2 cups low-fat milk
¼ teaspoon black pepper
¼ teaspoon salt
2 tablespoons chopped fresh parsley
6 slices bacon, well cooked, drained and crumbled (optional)

1. Pour broth into crock pot . 2. Add potatoes, onions, creamed corn, and carrot. 3. Cover. Cook on high 1 hour. Stir. Cook on high another hour. 4. Using a potato masher, mash potatoes coarsely to thicken soup. 5. Add clams, milk, salt, black pepper, salt, and parsley. 6. Cover. Cook on high 20 minutes. 7. Garnish with crumbled bacon, if desired.

Southwestern Beef and Veggie Stew

Prep time: 20 minutes | Cook time: 4½ to 6½ hours | Serves 4 to 6

2 pounds (907 g) sirloin or stewing meat, cubed
2 tablespoons oil
1 large onion, diced
2 garlic cloves, minced
1½ cups water
1 tablespoon dried parsley flakes
2 beef bouillon cubes
1 teaspoon ground cumin
½ teaspoon salt
3 carrots, sliced
1 (14½-ounce / 411-g) can
diced tomatoes
1 (14½-ounce / 411-g) can green beans, drained, or 1 pound (454 g) frozen green beans
1 (14½-ounce / 411-g) can corn, drained, or 1 pound (454 g) frozen corn
1 (4-ounce / 113-g) can diced green chilies
3 zucchini squash, diced (optional)

1. Brown meat, onion, and garlic in oil in saucepan until meat is no longer pink. Place in crock pot . 2. Stir in remaining ingredients. 3. Cover. Cook on high 30 minutes. Reduce heat to low and cook 4 to 6 hours.

Crab Meat Soup

Prep time: 10 minutes | Cook time: 5 to 6 hours | Serves 8

2 (10¾-ounce / 305-g) cans cream of tomato soup
2 (10½-ounce / 298-g) cans split pea soup
3 cans milk
1 cup heavy cream
1 or 2 (6-ounce / 170-g) cans crab meat, drained
¼ cup sherry (optional)

1. Pour the soups into the crock pot, then add the milk and stir until well combined. 2. Cover and cook on low for 4 hours, or until the mixture is hot. 3. Stir in the cream and crab meat, then cook for an additional hour on low until fully heated.

Herbed Turkey and Veggie Soup

Prep time: 15 minutes | Cook time: 8 hours | Serves 8

1 pound (454 g) 99% fat-free ground turkey
3 parsley stalks with leaves, sliced
3 scallions, chopped
3 medium carrots, unpeeled, sliced
3 medium potatoes, unpeeled, sliced
3 celery ribs with leaves
3 small onions, sliced
1 (1-pound / 454-g) can
whole-kernel corn with juice
1 (1-pound / 454-g) can green beans with juice
1 (1-pound / 454-g) can low-sodium diced Italian-style tomatoes
3 cans water
3 packets dry Herb-Ox vegetable broth
1 tablespoon crushed rosemary, fresh or dry

1. Brown turkey with parsley and scallions in iron skillet. Drain. Pour into crock pot sprayed with nonfat cooking spray. 2. Add vegetables, water, dry vegetable broth, and rosemary. 3. Cover. Cook on low 8 hours.

Mushroom-Beef Stew

Prep time: 20 minutes | Cook time: 6 to 7½ hours | Serves 8 to 10

1 pound (454 g) sirloin, cubed
2 tablespoons flour
Oil
1 large onion, chopped
2 garlic cloves, minced
½ pound (227 g) button
mushrooms, sliced
2 ribs celery, sliced
2 carrots, sliced
3 to 4 large potatoes, cubed
2 teaspoons seasoned salt
1 (14½-ounce / 411-g) can beef stock, or 2 bouillon

cubes dissolved in 1⅔ cups water
½ to 1 cup good red wine

1. Coat the sirloin in flour and brown it in a skillet, saving the drippings. Transfer the meat to the crock pot. 2. Sauté the onion, garlic, and mushrooms in the reserved drippings until softened, then add them to the meat in the crock pot. 3. Add all the remaining ingredients. 4. Cover and cook on low for 6 hours. Check the vegetables for tenderness, and if needed, cook for an additional 1 to 1½ hours on low. 5. Serve hot.

Coastal Harvest Crab Soup

Prep time: 20 minutes | Cook time: 8 to 10 hours | Serves 10

1 pound (454 g) carrots, sliced
½ bunch celery, sliced
1 large onion, diced
2 (10-ounce / 283-g) bags frozen mixed vegetables, or your choice of frozen vegetables
1 (12-ounce / 340-g) can tomato juice
1 pound (454 g) ham,
cubed
1 pound (454 g) beef, cubed
6 slices bacon, chopped
1 teaspoon salt
¼ teaspoon pepper
1 tablespoon Old Bay seasoning
1 pound (454 g) claw crab meat

1. Combine all ingredients except seasonings and crab meat in large crock pot . Pour in water until cooker is half-full. 2. Add spices. Stir in thoroughly. Put crab on top. 3. Cover. Cook on low 8 to 10 hours. 4. Stir well and serve.

Pork-Veggie Stew

Prep time: 15 minutes | Cook time: 6 hours | Serves 8

2 pounds (907 g) boneless pork loin, cut into 1-inch cubes
8 medium potatoes, peeled and cut into 2-inch pieces
6 large carrots, peeled and cut into 2-inch pieces
1 cup ketchup
2¼ cups water, divided

1. Brown the pork cubes in a large skillet over medium heat. 2. Lightly coat the crock pot with nonstick spray. 3. Add all ingredients to the crock pot, except for the ketchup and ¼ cup of water. 4. Cover and cook on high for 5 hours. One hour before serving, mix the ketchup with ¼ cup water and pour it over the stew. Cook for another hour.

Spicy Mexican Bean and Rice Soup

Prep time: 15 minutes | Cook time: 6 hours | Serves 6

½ cup chopped onions

⅓ cup chopped green peppers

1 garlic clove, minced

1 tablespoon oil

1 (4-ounce / 113-g) package sliced or chipped dried beef

1 (18-ounce / 510-g) can tomato juice

1 (15½-ounce / 439-g) can red kidney beans, undrained

1½ cups water

½ cup long-grain rice, uncooked

1 teaspoon paprika

½ to 1 teaspoon chili powder

½ teaspoon salt

Dash of pepper

1. Cook onions, green peppers, and garlic in oil in skillet until vegetables are tender but not brown. Transfer to crock pot . 2. Tear beef into small pieces and add to crock pot . 3. Add remaining ingredients. Mix well. 4. Cover. Cook on low 6 hours. Stir before serving. 5. Serve.

Lentil Soup with Ham

Prep time: 15 minutes | Cook time: 7 to 9 hours | Serves 8

1 cup chopped onions

3 cloves garlic, minced

5 cups fat-free, low-sodium chicken broth

1 cup dried lentils

½ cup chopped carrots

2 bay leaves

3 cups chopped Swiss chard

1½ cups chopped potatoes

1 cup chopped ham

1 (14½-ounce / 411-g) can low-sodium diced tomatoes

1 teaspoon dried basil

½ teaspoon dried thyme

½ teaspoon black pepper

3 tablespoons chopped fresh parsley

1. Place all ingredients in the crock pot, leaving out the fresh parsley. 2. Cover and cook on low for 7 to 9 hours. 3. Stir in the fresh parsley just before serving.

Sausage and Lentil Stew

Prep time: 10 minutes | Cook time: 4 to 6 hours | Serves 6

2 cups dry lentils, picked over and rinsed

1 (14½-ounce / 411-g) can diced tomatoes

8 cups canned chicken broth or water

1 tablespoon salt

½ to 1 pound (227 to 454 g) pork or beef sausage, cut into 2-inch pieces

1. Place lentils, tomatoes, chicken broth, and salt in crock pot . Stir to combine. Place sausage pieces on top. 2. Cover and cook on low 4 to 6 hours, or until lentils are tender but not dry or mushy.

Barley and Chicken Soup

Prep time: 10 minutes | Cook time: 4 to 6 hours | Serves 5

½ pound (227 g) dry barley

1 small soup chicken, cut up

Fresh celery, as desired

Parsley, as desired

Basil, as desired

Carrots, as desired

1. Add all the ingredients to the crock pot and cover with water. 2. Cover the pot and cook on low for 4 to 6 hours. 3. Remove the chicken from the bones, discard the skin, and return the meat to the soup. Continue cooking until the barley is tender.

Chapter 3

Poultry

Herb roasted chicken with root vegetables

Prep time: 30 minutes | Cook time: 6 hours | Serves 6

6 to 8 potatoes, quartered	1 tablespoon whole cloves
1 to 2 large onions, sliced	1 tablespoon garlic salt
3 to 5 carrots, cubed	1 tablespoon chopped fresh
1 (5-pound / 2.3-kg)	oregano
chicken, skin removed	1 teaspoon dried rosemary
1 small onion, chopped	½ cup lemon juice or
1 teaspoon black pepper	chicken broth

1. Layer potatoes, sliced onions, and carrots in bottom of crock pot . 2. Rinse and pat chicken dry. In bowl mix together chopped onions, pepper, cloves, and garlic salt. Dredge chicken in seasonings. Place in cooker over vegetables. Spoon any remaining seasonings over chicken. 3. Sprinkle with oregano and rosemary. Pour lemon juice over chicken. 4. Cover. Cook on low 6 hours.

Curried Chicken with Coconut and Basil

Prep time: 20 minutes | Cook time: 6 to 8 hours | Serves 6 to 8

4 tablespoons (½ stick) unsalted butter	apple, cored and cut into ½-inch dice
18 chicken thighs, boned and skinned	¼ cup all-purpose flour
1 teaspoon garam masala	2 cups chicken broth
2 medium onions, finely chopped	1½ teaspoons sweet curry powder
1 teaspoon freshly grated ginger	1 cup coconut milk
2 cloves garlic, minced	¼ cup finely chopped fresh basil
1 large Granny Smith	Steamed rice for serving

1. Heat 2 tablespoons of butter in a large skillet over high heat. Sprinkle the chicken thighs with garam masala, and cook them in batches, browning all sides. Transfer the browned chicken to the insert of a 5- to 7-quart crock pot. In the same skillet, add the onions, ginger, garlic, and apple, sautéing over medium-high heat until the onions begin to soften, about 5 minutes. Transfer everything from the skillet into the crock pot. 2. Melt the remaining 2 tablespoons of butter in the skillet. Add the flour and cook, whisking constantly for 3 minutes. Gradually add the chicken broth and bring the mixture to a boil. 3. Stir in the curry powder and coconut milk, then pour the sauce into the crock pot. Cover and cook on low for 6 to 8 hours, or until the chicken is tender. Stir in the basil just before serving. 4. Serve the curry over a bed of steamed rice.

Noodleless Lasagna

Prep time: 20 minutes | Cook time: 4 to 4½ hours | Serves 4

1½ pounds (680 g) fat-free ground turkey	1 egg, beaten
1½ cups meat-free, low-sodium spaghetti sauce	1 cup shredded Mozzarella cheese (part skim), divided
8 ounces (227 g) sliced mushrooms	1½ teaspoons Italian seasoning
1½ cups fat-free ricotta cheese	10 slices turkey pepperoni
	Nonfat cooking spray

1. Brown the ground turkey in a nonstick skillet, breaking it up as it cooks. 2. Stir in the spaghetti sauce and mushrooms, mixing them with the turkey. 3. Spray the crock pot with nonfat cooking spray and add half of the turkey mixture, spreading it evenly. 4. In a small bowl, combine the ricotta cheese, egg, ¼ cup of Mozzarella, and Italian seasoning. Beat well with a fork until smooth. 5. Layer half of the pepperoni slices over the turkey mixture. 6. Spread half of the cheese mixture over the pepperoni. 7. Repeat the layering process, finishing with the remaining Mozzarella on top. 8. Cover and cook on low for 4 to 4½ hours, until bubbly and heated through.

Hearty chicken pot pie stew

Prep time: 15 minutes | Cook time: 8 hours | Serves 2

2 boneless, skinless chicken thighs, diced	⅛ teaspoon sea salt
1 cup diced, peeled Yukon Gold potatoes	Freshly ground black pepper
1 cup frozen peas, thawed	1 tablespoon all-purpose flour
1 cup diced onions	1 cup low-sodium chicken broth
1 cup diced carrots	
1 teaspoon fresh thyme	

1. Put the chicken, potatoes, peas, onions, carrots, and thyme in the crock pot . Season with the salt and a few grinds of the pepper. Sprinkle in the flour and toss to coat the chicken and vegetables. Pour in the chicken broth. 2. Cover and cook on low for 8 hours.

Turkey Meat Loaf

Prep time: 15 minutes | Cook time: 6 to 8 hours | Serves 8

1½ pounds (680 g) lean ground turkey
2 egg whites
⅓ cup ketchup
1 tablespoon Worcestershire sauce
1 teaspoon dried basil
½ teaspoon salt
½ teaspoon black pepper
2 small onions, chopped
2 potatoes, finely shredded
2 small red bell peppers, finely chopped

1. Mix all the ingredients together in a large bowl. 2. Shape the mixture into a loaf that will fit in your crock pot and place it inside. 3. Cover and cook on low for 6 to 8 hours until fully cooked.

Ginger soy chicken

Prep time: 10 minutes | Cook time: 7 to 8 hours | Serves 6

6 to 8 skinless chicken thighs
½ cup soy sauce
2 tablespoons brown sugar
2 tablespoons grated fresh ginger
2 garlic cloves, minced

1. Wash and dry chicken. Place in crock pot . 2. Combine remaining ingredients. Pour over chicken. 3. Cover. Cook on high 1 hour. Reduce heat to low and cook 6 to 7 hours. 4. Serve.

Cumin-Spiced Chicken Wings

Prep time: 10 minutes | Cook time: 4 to 6 hours | Serves 6

3 tablespoons rapeseed oil
2 teaspoons ground cumin seeds, ground
2 teaspoons crushed garlic
2 teaspoons freshly grated ginger
1 teaspoon cumin seeds
1 teaspoon salt
1 teaspoon coriander seeds, ground
1 teaspoon chili powder
2 fresh green chiles, finely sliced
24 chicken wings
Handful fresh coriander leaves, chopped
Juice of 1 lemon
1 teaspoon red chili flakes (optional)

1. Preheat the crock pot on the high setting. 2. In a bowl, combine all the ingredients except the coriander leaves, lemon juice, and chili flakes. Add the wings and toss them to coat evenly. 3. Place the wings in the crock pot, cover, and cook on low for 6 hours or on high for 4 hours. 4. When ready to serve, garnish with fresh coriander leaves, a squeeze of lemon, and chili flakes if desired.

Stuffed Pepper Medley

Prep time: 20 minutes | Cook time: 3 to 9 hours | Serves 8

8 small green peppers, tops removed and seeded
1 (10-ounce / 283-g) package frozen corn
¾ pound (340 g) 99% fat-free ground turkey
¾ pound (340 g) extra-lean ground beef
1 (8-ounce / 227-g) can low-sodium tomato sauce
½ teaspoon garlic powder
¼ teaspoon black pepper
1 cup shredded low-fat American cheese
½ teaspoon Worcestershire sauce
¼ cup chopped onions
3 tablespoons water
2 tablespoons ketchup

1. Wash peppers and drain well. Combine all ingredients except water and ketchup in mixing bowl. Stir well. 2. Stuff peppers ⅔ full. 3. Pour water in crock pot . Arrange peppers on top. 4. Pour ketchup over peppers. 5. Cover. Cook on high 3 to 4 hours, or on low 7 to 9 hours.

Chicken veggie melt

Prep time: 15 minutes | Cook time: 7 hours | Serves 2

1 onion, sliced
2 garlic cloves, sliced
1 carrot, slivered
1 red bell pepper, chopped
5 boneless, skinless chicken thighs
½ teaspoon salt
½ teaspoon dried thyme leaves
⅛ teaspoon freshly ground black pepper
¼ cup chicken stock
2 crusty sandwich rolls, split and toasted
2 tablespoons mayonnaise
2 tablespoons grainy mustard

1. In the crock pot , combine the onion, garlic, carrot, and red bell pepper. 2. On a platter, sprinkle the chicken with the salt, thyme, and pepper, and place the chicken on top of the vegetables in the crock pot . Pour the stock over everything. 3. Cover and cook on low for 7 hours, or until the chicken registers 165ºF (74ºC) on a meat thermometer. 4. Remove the chicken from the crock pot to a clean platter and shred. Return the meat to the crock pot and stir. 5. Make sandwiches with the rolls, mayonnaise, and mustard, and serve.

Zesty Chicken Breasts

Prep time: 15 minutes | Cook time: 3 to 8 hours | Serves 6

6 bone-in chicken breast halves
2 (14½-ounce / 411-g) cans diced tomatoes, undrained
1 small can jalapeños, sliced and drained (optional)
¼ cup reduced-fat, creamy peanut butter
2 tablespoons fresh cilantro, chopped (optional)
Nonfat cooking spray

1. Remove the skin from the chicken, keeping the bones intact. 2. In a medium-sized bowl, mix all the ingredients, except for the chicken. 3. Spray the bottom of the crock pot with nonfat cooking spray and pour one-third of the sauce into the pot. Place the chicken on top. 4. Pour the remaining sauce over the chicken. 5. Cover and cook on high for 3 to 4 hours, or on low for 6 to 8 hours. 6. Gently remove the chicken from the crock pot, as it will be very tender and may fall off the bones.

Rosemary lemon glazed wings

Prep time: 20 minutes | Cook time: 3 hours | Serves 8

3 pounds (1.4 kg) chicken wing drumettes
¼ cup olive oil
1½ teaspoons salt
1 teaspoon sweet paprika
Freshly ground black pepper
Sauce:
½ cup lemon juice
Grated zest of 3 lemons
2 teaspoons salt
Pinch of red pepper flakes
½ cup extra-virgin olive oil
2 tablespoons red wine vinegar
6 cloves garlic, minced
1 tablespoon finely minced fresh rosemary
½ cup chicken broth

1. Coat the insert of a 5- to 7-quart crock pot with nonstick cooking spray. Preheat the broiler for 10 minutes. 2. Combine the wings, olive oil, salt, paprika, and a generous grinding of pepper in a large mixing bowl and toss until the wings are evenly coated. Arrange the wings on a wire rack in a baking sheet and broil until the wings are crispy on one side, about 5 minutes. 3. Turn the wings and broil until crispy and browned an additional 5 minutes. 4. Remove the wings from the oven. If you would like to do this step ahead of time, cool the wings and refrigerate for up to 2 days. Otherwise, put the wings in the prepared cooker insert. 5. Combine all the sauce ingredients in a mixing bowl and stir. Pour the sauce over the wings and turn to coat. 6. Cover and cook on high for 3 hours, turning the wings several times to coat with the sauce. 7. Serve the wings from the cooker set on warm.

Chicken tortilla bake

Prep time: 25 minutes | Cook time: 3 to 6 hours | Serves 8 to 10

4 whole boneless, skinless chicken breasts, cooked and cut in 1-inch pieces (reserve ¼ cup broth chicken was cooked in)
10 (6-inch) flour tortillas, cut in strips about ½-inch wide × 2-inches long
2 medium onions, chopped
1 teaspoon canola oil
1 (10¾-ounce / 305-g) can fat-free chicken broth
1 (10¾-ounce / 305-g) can 98% fat-free cream of mushroom soup
2 (4-ounce / 113-g) cans mild green chilies, chopped
1 egg
1 cup shredded low-fat Cheddar cheese

1. Pour reserved chicken broth in crock pot sprayed with nonfat cooking spray. 2. Scatter half the tortilla strips in bottom of crock pot . 3. Mix remaining ingredients together, except the second half of the tortilla strips and the cheese. 4. Layer half the chicken mixture into the cooker, followed by the other half of the tortillas, followed by the rest of the chicken mix. 5. Cover. Cook on low 4 to 6 hours, or on high 3 to 5 hours. 6. Add the cheese to the top of the dish during the last 20 to 30 minutes of cooking. 7. Uncover and allow casserole to rest 15 minutes before serving.

Chicken and Shrimp Casserole

Prep time: 20 minutes | Cook time: 3 to 8 hours | Serves 6

1¼ cups rice, uncooked
2 tablespoons butter, melted
3 cups fat-free, low-sodium chicken broth
1 cup water
3 cups cut-up, cooked skinless chicken breast
2 (4-ounce / 113-g) cans
sliced mushrooms, drained
⅓ cup light soy sauce
1 (12-ounce / 340-g) package shelled frozen shrimp
8 green onions, chopped, 2 tablespoons reserved
⅔ cup slivered almonds

1. Place the rice and butter in the crock pot and stir to coat the rice evenly. 2. Add the remaining ingredients, reserving the almonds and 2 tablespoons of green onions. 3. Cover and cook on low for 6 to 8 hours, or on high for 3 to 4 hours, until the rice is tender. 4. Before serving, sprinkle the almonds and green onions over the top.

Roasted Red Pepper and Mozzarella Stuffed Chicken Breasts

Prep time: 15 minutes | Cook time: 6 to 8 hours | Serves 2

1 teaspoon extra-virgin olive oil
2 boneless, skinless chicken breasts
⅛ teaspoon sea salt
Freshly ground black pepper

2 roasted red bell peppers, cut into thin strips
2 ounces (57 g) sliced mozzarella cheese
¼ cup roughly chopped fresh basil

1. Lightly grease the inside of the crock pot with olive oil. 2. Slice the chicken breasts horizontally through the center, but not all the way through—open them like a book. Season both sides with salt and pepper. 3. On one half of each chicken breast, layer the roasted peppers, followed by the mozzarella slices. Sprinkle fresh basil on top of the cheese, then fold the other half of the chicken over the filling. 4. Carefully place the stuffed chicken breasts into the crock pot, ensuring the filling stays inside. Cover and cook on low for 6 to 8 hours, or until the chicken is fully cooked.

Barbecued Turkey

Prep time: 15 minutes | Cook time: 3 to 4 hours | Serves 6

3 large onions, coarsely chopped
2 red bell peppers, seeded and coarsely chopped
1 (4-pound / 1.8-kg) bone-in turkey breast, skin removed
1 cup ketchup

1 cup tomato sauce
½ cup Dijon mustard
¼ cup firmly packed light brown sugar
2 tablespoons Worcestershire sauce
½ teaspoon Tabasco sauce

1. Place the onions and bell peppers at the bottom of the insert of a 5- to 7-quart crock pot, then lay the turkey breast on top of the vegetables. In a small bowl, mix together the ketchup, tomato sauce, mustard, sugar, Worcestershire sauce, and Tabasco. 2. Brush some of the barbecue sauce over the turkey breast, then pour the remaining sauce over the turkey and vegetables in the crock pot. Cover and cook on high for 3 to 4 hours, or until the turkey reaches an internal temperature of 175ºF (79ºC) on an instant-read thermometer. 3. Carefully remove the turkey from the crock pot, cover with aluminum foil, and let it rest for 20 minutes before carving. 4. Strain the sauce through a fine-mesh sieve into a bowl, discarding the solids. Return the sauce to the crock pot. 5. Carve the turkey and serve with the sauce, or return the turkey to the crock pot with the sauce and serve from the pot on warm.

Coconut Curry Chicken

Prep time: 15 minutes | Cook time: 3 to 4 hours | Serves 6

1 tablespoon coconut oil
1 teaspoon cumin seeds
2 medium onions, grated
7 to 8 ounces (198 to 227 g) canned plum tomatoes
1 teaspoon salt
1 teaspoon turmeric
½ to 1 teaspoon Kashmiri chili powder (optional)

2 to 3 fresh green chiles, chopped
1 cup coconut cream
12 chicken thighs, skinned, trimmed, and cut into bite-size chunks
1 teaspoon garam masala
Handful fresh coriander leaves, chopped

1. Heat the oil in a frying pan (or in the crock pot if it has a sear setting). Add the cumin seeds and cook until they start to sizzle and become aromatic. Then, add the onions and cook for about 5 to 7 minutes until they begin to brown. 2. Purée the tomatoes in a blender and add them to the pan with the salt, turmeric, chili powder (if using), and fresh green chiles. Stir everything together. 3. Transfer the mixture to the crock pot. Add the coconut cream and the meat, stirring to coat the meat in the sauce. 4. Cover and cook on low for 4 hours, or on high for 3 hours. 5. Taste the sauce and adjust the seasoning. If the sauce is too liquid, set the crock pot to high and cook for an additional 30 minutes with the lid off to thicken. 6. Stir in the garam masala and sprinkle fresh coriander leaves before serving.

Basic Poached Chicken Breasts

Prep time: 15 minutes | Cook time: 4 to 5 hours | Serves 8

2 cups chicken broth
3 whole black peppercorns
½ teaspoon dried thyme

12 chicken breast halves, skin and bones removed

1. In the insert of a 5- to 7-quart crock pot, combine the broth, peppercorns, and thyme. Arrange the chicken breasts in a single layer in the pot. 2. Cover and cook on low for 4 to 5 hours, or until the chicken is cooked through and tender. Once done, let the chicken cool before removing it from the crock pot. Refrigerate for up to 2 days or freeze for up to 10 weeks.

Creamy chicken broccoli rice

Prep time: 20 minutes | Cook time: 6 to 8 hours | Serves 6

1¼ cups long-grain rice, uncooked
Pepper to taste
2 pounds (907 g) boneless, skinless chicken breasts,
cut into strips
1 package Knorr's cream of broccoli dry soup mix
2½ cups chicken broth
Nonstick cooking spray

1. Spray crock pot with nonstick cooking spray. Place rice in cooker. Sprinkle with pepper. 2. Top with chicken pieces. 3. In a mixing bowl, combine soup mix and broth. Pour over chicken and rice. 4. Cover and cook on low 6 to 8 hours, or until rice and chicken are tender but not dry.

Chicken and biscuit stew

Prep time: 10 minutes | Cook time: 2½ hours | Serves 5 to 6

1 pound (454 g) boneless, skinless chicken breasts, uncooked and cut in 1-inch cubes
1 pound (454 g) frozen vegetables of your choice
1 medium onion, diced
2 (12-ounce / 340-g) jars fat-free low-sodium chicken broth, divided
1½ cups low-fat buttermilk biscuit mix

1. Combine chicken, vegetables, onion, and chicken broth (reserve ½ cup, plus 1 tablespoon, broth) in crock pot . 2. Cover. Cook on high 2 hours. 3. Mix biscuit mix with reserved broth until moistened. Drop by tablespoonfuls over hot chicken and vegetables. 4. Cover. Cook on high 10 minutes. 5. Uncover. Cook on high 20 minutes more.

Balsamic fig chicken

Prep time: 15 minutes | Cook time: 2 hours | Serves 6 to 8

2 tablespoons vegetable oil
8 chicken breast halves, skin and bones removed
1½ teaspoons salt
½ teaspoon freshly ground black pepper
½ cup balsamic vinegar
½ cup Ruby Port
½ cup chicken broth
1 teaspoon dried thyme
16 dried figs, cut in half

1. Heat the oil in a large skillet over medium-high heat. Sprinkle the chicken evenly with the salt and pepper. 2. Add the chicken to the skillet and brown on all sides. 3. Transfer the chicken to the insert of a 5- to 7-quart crock pot . Deglaze the pan with the vinegar and port, scraping up any browned bits from the bottom of the pan. Add the broth and transfer the contents of the skillet to the crock pot . 4. Add the thyme and figs and stir to combine. Cover and cook on high for 2 hours, until the chicken is cooked through and the sauce is syrupy. 5. Serve the chicken from the cooker set on warm.

Gran's hearty meat and vegetable stew

Prep time: 20 minutes | Cook time: 10 to 12 hours | Serves 10 to 15

2½ to 3 pounds (1.1 to 1.4 kg) stewing hen, cut into pieces
½ pound (227 g) stewing beef, cubed
1 (½-pound / 227-g) veal shoulder or roast, cubed
1½ quarts water
½ pound (227 g) small red potatoes, cubed
½ pound (227 g) small onions, cut in half
1 cup sliced carrots
1 cup chopped celery
1 green pepper, chopped
1 (1-pound / 454-g) package frozen lima beans
1 cup fresh or frozen okra
1 cup whole-kernel corn
1 (8-ounce / 227-g) can whole tomatoes with juice
1 (15-ounce / 425-g) can tomato purée
1 teaspoon salt
¼ to ½ teaspoon pepper
1 teaspoon dry mustard
½ teaspoon chili powder
¼ cup chopped fresh parsley

1. Combine all ingredients except last 5 seasonings in one very large crock pot , or divide between two medium-sized ones. 2. Cover. Cook on low 10 to 12 hours. Add seasonings during last hour of cooking.

Barbecue Chicken for Buns

Prep time: 15 minutes | Cook time: 8 hours | Serves 16 to 20

6 cups diced cooked chicken
2 cups chopped celery
1 cup chopped onions
1 cup chopped green peppers
4 tablespoons butter
2 cups ketchup
2 cups water
2 tablespoons brown sugar
4 tablespoons vinegar
2 teaspoons dry mustard
1 teaspoon pepper
1 teaspoon salt

1. Add all the ingredients to the crock pot. 2. Cover and cook on low for 8 hours. 3. Shred the chicken with a fork once it's cooked through. 4. Serve as desired.

Sweet Potatoes and Chicken Curry

Prep time: 10 minutes | Cook time: 5¼ to 6¼ hours | Serves 4

4 boneless, skinless chicken breast halves
1 small onion, chopped
2 sweet potatoes (about 1½ pounds / 680 g), cubed
⅔ cup orange juice
1 garlic clove, minced
1 teaspoon chicken bouillon granules
1 teaspoon salt
¼ teaspoon pepper
4 teaspoons curry powder
2 tablespoons cornstarch
2 tablespoons cold water
Sliced green onions
Shredded coconut
Peanuts
Raisins

1. Place the chicken in the crock pot and top with onions and sweet potatoes. 2. In a bowl, mix together the orange juice, garlic, chicken bouillon, salt, pepper, and curry powder. Pour the mixture over the vegetables. 3. Cover and cook on low for 5 to 6 hours. 4. Remove the chicken and vegetables, keeping them warm. 5. Set the crock pot to high. Dissolve the cornstarch in cold water and stir it into the sauce. Cover and cook on high for 15 to 20 minutes. 6. Serve the dish topped with your choice of remaining ingredients.

Cilantro peanut chicken thighs

Prep time: 5 minutes | Cook time: 2½ hours | Serves 4 to 6

2 tablespoons extra-virgin olive oil
2 onions, coarsely chopped
2½ pounds (1.1 kg) boneless, skinless chicken thighs, cut into 1½-inch pieces
Coarse salt and freshly ground pepper
1 tablespoon minced peeled fresh ginger
5 garlic cloves, thinly sliced
1 jalapeño chile (ribs and seeds removed for less heat, if desired), thinly sliced, plus more for serving
4 cups packed fresh cilantro, plus more for garnish
½ cup roasted peanuts, plus more, chopped, for serving
2 teaspoons light brown sugar
1 tablespoon fresh lime juice, plus wedges for serving

1. Preheat a 5- to 6-quart crock pot . 2. Heat a large skillet over medium-high. Add oil and onions; cook, stirring occasionally, until browned, about 8 minutes. Transfer to the crock pot . 3. Season chicken with salt and pepper; add to crock pot along with ginger, garlic, and jalapeño. Cover and cook on high until chicken is tender, 2 hours (or on low for 4 hours). 4. In a food processor, pulse cilantro, peanuts, brown sugar, and lime juice just until finely chopped (do not process to a paste); transfer to crock pot . Cover and continue to cook on high 30 minutes (or on low for 1 hour). Season with salt and pepper. Serve with jalapeño, cilantro, peanuts, and lime wedges.

Chicken and shrimp gumbo

Prep time: 45 minutes | Cook time: 10 to 12 hours | Serves 12

1 cup chopped celery
1 cup chopped onions
½ cup chopped green peppers
¼ cup olive oil
¼ cup, plus 1 tablespoon, flour
6 cups chicken stock
2 pounds (907 g) chicken, cut up
3 bay leaves
1½ cups sliced okra
1 (12-ounce / 340-g) can diced tomatoes
1 teaspoon Tabasco sauce
Salt to taste
Pepper to taste
1 pound (454 g) ready-to-eat shrimp
½ cup snipped fresh parsley

1. Sauté celery, onions, and peppers in oil. Blend in flour and chicken stock until smooth. Cook 5 minutes. Pour into crock pot . 2. Add remaining ingredients except seafood and parsley. 3. Cover. Cook on low 10 to 12 hours. 4. One hour before serving add shrimp and parsley. 5. Remove bay leaves before serving. 6. Serve.

Chicken at a Whim

Prep time: 10 minutes | Cook time: 4½ hours | Serves 6 to 8

6 medium, boneless, skinless chicken breast halves
1 small onion, sliced
1 cup dry white wine, chicken broth, or water
1 (15-ounce / 425-g) can chicken broth
2 cups water
1 (6-ounce / 170-g) can
sliced black olives, with juice
1 small can artichoke hearts, with juice
5 garlic cloves, minced
1 cup dry elbow macaroni or small shells
1 envelope dry savory garlic soup

1. Add the chicken to the crock pot and spread the onion over it. 2. Mix the remaining ingredients (excluding the dry soup mix) and pour over the chicken. Sprinkle the dry soup mix on top. 3. Cover and cook on low for 4½ hours.

White Chicken Chili

Prep time: 25 minutes | Cook time: 3½ to 5 hours | Serves 6 to 8

2 whole skinless chicken breasts
6 cups water
2 chopped onions
2 garlic cloves, minced
1 tablespoon oil
2 to 4 (4-ounce / 113-g) cans chopped green chilies
1 to 2 diced jalapeño peppers

2 teaspoons ground cumin
1½ teaspoons dried oregano
¼ teaspoon cayenne pepper
½ teaspoon salt
1 (3-pound / 1.4-kg) can navy beans, undrained
1 to 2 cups shredded cheese
Sour cream
Salsa

1. Start by placing the chicken in the crock pot and adding 6 cups of water to cover it. 2. Cover and cook on low for 3 to 4 hours, until the chicken is cooked through and tender. 3. Once done, remove the chicken from the crock pot, cube it, and set it aside for later. 4. In a skillet, heat oil and sauté the onions and garlic until softened. Add the chilies, jalapeños, cumin, oregano, pepper, and salt. Sauté for about 2 minutes, then transfer this mixture into the crock pot with the broth. 5. Stir in the navy beans, making sure they are well combined. 6. Cover the crock pot again and cook on low for an additional 30 to 60 minutes. 7. Just before serving, add the cubed chicken and cheese, stirring gently until the cheese melts. 8. Serve the dish topped with a dollop of sour cream and a spoonful of salsa for extra flavor.

Chicken and Apples

Prep time: 20 minutes | Cook time: 7 to 8 hours | Serves 6

1 (6-ounce / 170-g) can frozen orange concentrate, thawed
½ teaspoon dried marjoram leaves
Dash ground nutmeg
Dash garlic powder

1 onion, chopped
6 skinless, boneless chicken breast halves
3 Granny Smith apples, cored and sliced
¼ cup water
2 tablespoons cornstarch

1. In a small bowl, whisk together the orange juice concentrate, marjoram, nutmeg, and garlic powder until well blended. 2. Layer the onions in the bottom of the crock pot. 3. Dip each chicken breast into the orange mixture, coating it thoroughly before placing it in the crock pot on top of the onions. 4. Pour any remaining orange mixture over the chicken, ensuring it's well-covered. 5. Cover the crock pot and cook on low for 6 to 7 hours, or until the chicken is fully cooked. 6. Add the apples to the crock pot and continue to cook for another hour on low. 7. Once done, carefully remove the chicken, apples, and onions from the crock pot and place them on a serving platter. 8. Transfer the remaining sauce from the crock pot into a medium saucepan. 9. In a small bowl, mix water and cornstarch until smooth, then stir the mixture into the sauce. 10. Cook the sauce over medium heat, stirring constantly until it thickens and becomes bubbly. 11. Pour the thickened sauce over the chicken and serve.

Crocked Stuffing with Poultry

Prep time: 15 minutes | Cook time: 7 to 9 hours | Serves 18

1 large loaf dried low-fat bread, cubed
2 cups chopped, cooked turkey or chicken, skin removed
1 large onion, chopped
3 ribs celery with leaves, chopped

¼ cup butter, melted
4 cups fat-free chicken broth
1 tablespoon poultry seasoning
1 teaspoon salt
4 eggs, beaten
½ teaspoon black pepper

1. Combine all the ingredients and pour the mixture into the crock pot. 2. Cover and cook on high for 1 hour, then reduce the heat to low and cook for 6 to 8 hours.

Turkey-Pumpkin Ragout

Prep time: 15 minutes | Cook time: 8 hours | Serves 6

1 tablespoon extra-virgin olive oil
1 pound (454 g) boneless turkey thighs, cut into 1½-inch chunks
3 cups cubed pumpkin, cut into 1-inch chunks
1 red bell pepper, diced
½ sweet onion, cut in half and sliced
1 tablespoon minced garlic

1½ cups chicken broth
1½ cups coconut milk
2 teaspoons chopped fresh thyme
½ cup coconut cream
Salt, for seasoning
Freshly ground black pepper, for seasoning
12 slices cooked bacon, chopped, for garnish

1. Coat the insert of the crock pot with olive oil. 2. Add the turkey, pumpkin, red bell pepper, onion, garlic, broth, coconut milk, and thyme. 3. Cover and cook on low for 8 hours. 4. Stir in the coconut cream and adjust the seasoning with salt and pepper. 5. Serve the dish with a topping of bacon.

Creamy chicken with peppers

Prep time: 15 minutes | Cook time: 4 to 5 hours | Serves 8

4 boneless, skinless chicken breast halves
4 skinless chicken quarters
1 (10¾-ounce / 305-g) can cream of chicken soup
1 tablespoon water
¼ cup chopped sweet red peppers
1 tablespoon chopped fresh parsley, or 1 teaspoon dried parsley (optional)
1 tablespoon lemon juice
½ teaspoon paprika (optional)

1. Layer chicken in crock pot . 2. Combine remaining ingredients and pour over chicken. Make sure all pieces are covered with sauce. 3. Cover. Cook on high 4 to 5 hours.

Chicken meatballs in marinara

Prep time: 45 minutes | Cook time: 5 to 7 hours | Serves 6 to 8

Quick Marinara:
2 tablespoons extra-virgin olive oil
1 medium onion, finely chopped
2 cloves garlic, minced
Pinch red pepper flakes (optional)
1 teaspoon dried basil
2 (28- to 32-ounce / 794- to 907-g) cans crushed tomatoes, with their juice
1½ teaspoons salt
1 teaspoon freshly ground black pepper
½ cups finely chopped fresh Italian parsley

Chicken Meatballs:
¼ cup milk
1 cup fresh bread crumbs
½ cup freshly grated Parmesan cheese
2 tablespoons finely chopped fresh Italian parsley
½ cup finely chopped onion
1 clove garlic, minced
1½ teaspoons salt
½ teaspoon freshly ground black pepper
2 pounds (907 g) ground chicken or turkey
1 large egg, beaten

1. Heat the oil in a small sauté pan over medium-high heat. Add the onion, garlic, red pepper flakes (if using), and basil and sauté until the onion is softened and begins to turn translucent, about 5 minutes. 2. Transfer the mixture to the insert of a 5- to 7-quart crock pot . Add the tomatoes, salt, pepper, and parsley to the cooker and stir to combine. 3. Cover and cook on low for 2 to 4 hours while making the meatballs. 4. Put the milk and the bread crumbs in a large mixing bowl and stir to combine. Add the remaining ingredients and stir until well combined. 5. Form the mixture into 2-inch balls and transfer them to the slow-cooker insert. Spoon some of the sauce over the meatballs.

6. Cover and cook on high for 3 hours, until the meatballs are cooked through and register 175ºF (79ºC) on an instant-read thermometer. Skim off any fat from the top of the sauce. 7. Serve the meatballs from the cooker set on warm.

Sweet and sour chicken with peppers

Prep time: 20 minutes | Cook time: 6 to 8 hours | Serves 4

Cooking spray or 1 tablespoon extra-virgin olive oil
1 medium onion, chopped
2 tablespoons minced garlic (about 6 cloves)
1 green bell pepper, seeded and roughly chopped
1 red bell pepper, seeded and roughly chopped
1 pound (454 g) boneless, skinless chicken thighs, cut into ½-inch cubes
¼ cup or low-sodium chicken stock
3 tablespoons packed brown sugar
3 tablespoons rice vinegar
½ teaspoon kosher salt, plus more for seasoning
½ teaspoon ground white pepper, plus more for seasoning
1 (8-ounce / 227-g) can pineapple chunks, drained
4 teaspoons cornstarch, mixed with 4 teaspoons water

1. Use the cooking spray or olive oil to coat the inside (bottom and sides) of the crock pot . Add the onion, garlic, bell peppers, chicken, chicken stock, brown sugar, vinegar, salt, and pepper. Stir to combine. Cover and cook on low for 6 to 8 hours. 2. About 30 minutes before serving, stir together the pineapple and cornstarch in a medium bowl until well combined. Add the mixture to the crock pot , stir to combine, cover, and continue cooking until the sauce begins to thicken. 3. Season with additional salt and pepper, as needed.

Salsa chicken with rice

Prep time: 5 minutes | Cook time: 6½ hours | Serves 8

8 boneless, skinless chicken breast halves
1 (16-ounce / 454-g) jar
salsa
2 cups instant rice

1. Place chicken in crock pot . Pour salsa over chicken. 2. Cover and cook on low 6 hours, or until chicken is tender but not dry. 3. Remove chicken to a serving platter and keep warm. 4. Add rice to hot salsa in crock pot and cook on high 30 minutes. Serve chicken and rice together on a large platter.

Mexican chicken tortilla soup

Prep time: 10 minutes | Cook time: 8 hours | Serves 6 to 8

4 chicken breast halves	heat
2 (15-ounce / 425-g) cans black beans, undrained	1 (4-ounce / 113-g) can chopped green chilies
2 (15-ounce / 425-g) cans Mexican stewed tomatoes, or Rotel tomatoes	1 (14½-ounce / 411-g) can tomato sauce
1 cup salsa, your choice of	Tortilla chips
	2 cups shredded cheese

1. Combine all ingredients except chips and cheese in large crock pot . 2. Cover. Cook on low 8 hours. 3. Just before serving, remove chicken breasts and slice into bite-sized pieces. Stir into soup. 4. To serve, put a handful of chips in each individual soup bowl. Ladle soup over chips. Top with cheese.

Spanish Chicken

Prep time: 10 minutes | Cook time: 8 hours | Serves 2

2 bone-in, skinless chicken quarters	⅔ cup long grain brown rice
2 teaspoons chili powder	1 (14 ounces / 397 g) can diced tomatoes, undrained
½ teaspoon ground sweet paprika	1 cup chicken stock
½ teaspoon salt	1 tablespoon freshly squeezed lemon juice
⅛ teaspoon ground cayenne pepper	½ teaspoon lemon zest
1 onion, chopped	1 pinch saffron threads
1 green bell pepper, chopped	¼ cup sliced green olives
2 garlic cloves, minced	1 cup frozen green peas, thawed

1. On a large platter, season the chicken quarters by sprinkling them evenly with chili powder, paprika, salt, and cayenne pepper. Rub the spices into the chicken to ensure it's well coated. 2. In the crock pot, combine the chopped onion, bell pepper, minced garlic, and uncooked rice. Place the seasoned chicken quarters on top of the rice mixture. 3. In a medium-sized bowl, mix together the diced tomatoes, chicken stock, lemon juice, lemon zest, and saffron. Let the mixture stand for 5 minutes to allow the saffron to bloom. Then, pour the tomato mixture over the chicken and rice in the crock pot. Top with the olives. 4. Cover the crock pot and cook on low for 7 to 8 hours, or until the chicken reaches an internal temperature of 165ºF (74ºC). 5. About 10 minutes before serving, add the frozen peas to the crock pot, stir them in, and cook on high for an additional 10 minutes until the peas are heated through. Serve hot and enjoy!

Lemon Chicken

Prep time: 20 minutes | Cook time: 3½ to 4½ hours | Serves 6

6 boneless, skinless chicken breast halves	3 tablespoons lemon juice
1 teaspoon dried oregano	2 garlic cloves, minced
½ teaspoon seasoned salt	2 teaspoons chicken bouillon granules
¼ teaspoon black pepper	2 teaspoons fresh parsley, minced
¼ cup water	

1. Pat the chicken dry using paper towels. 2. Mix together the oregano, seasoned salt, and pepper. Rub the seasoning mixture over the chicken. 3. Brown the chicken in a nonstick skillet over medium heat until lightly browned. 4. Transfer the browned chicken to the crock pot. 5. In the same skillet, combine water, lemon juice, garlic, and bouillon. Bring to a boil, stirring to loosen any browned bits. Pour this mixture over the chicken in the crock pot. 6. Cover and cook on low for 3 to 4 hours. 7. Baste the chicken with the cooking liquid and sprinkle with parsley. 8. Remove the lid and cook for an additional 15 to 30 minutes to allow the juices to thicken slightly. 9. Serve the chicken with the sauce.

Herb roasted Cornish hens with vegetables

Prep time: 15 minutes | Cook time: 8 hours | Serves 2

2 Cornish hens	1 cup sliced cremini mushrooms
½ teaspoon salt	2 carrots, sliced
½ teaspoon poultry seasoning	1 onion, chopped
⅛ teaspoon freshly ground black pepper	2 garlic cloves, minced
1 small lemon, cut into eighths	2 Yukon Gold potatoes, cubed
	½ cup chicken stock

1. On a platter, sprinkle the hens with the salt, poultry seasoning, and pepper. Stuff the lemon slices into the hens' cavities and set aside. 2. In the crock pot , combine the mushrooms, carrots, onion, garlic, and potatoes. Top with the hens and pour the stock over everything. 3. Cover and cook on low for 8 hours, or until the hens register 165ºF (74ºC) on a meat thermometer. 4. Serve the hens with the vegetables.

Jerk chicken with mango sauce

Prep time: 15 minutes | Cook time: 2½ to 3 hours | Serves 8

2 teaspoons jerk seasoning
1½ cups mango nectar
½ cup firmly packed light brown sugar

2 tablespoons dark corn syrup
2 tablespoons rice vinegar
8 chicken breast halves, skin and bones removed

1. Add the jerk seasoning, nectar, sugar, corn syrup, and rice vinegar to the insert of a 5- to 7-quart crock pot and stir to combine. 2. Add the chicken breasts and turn to coat in the sauce. Cover and cook on high for 2½ to 3 hours, until the chicken is cooked through. 3. Serve the chicken hot, warm, or at room temperature.

Punjabi Chicken Curry

Prep time: 20 minutes | Cook time: 4 to 6 hours | Serves 6

2 tablespoons vegetable oil
3 onions, finely diced
6 garlic cloves, finely chopped
1 heaped tablespoon freshly grated ginger
1 (14-ounce / 397-g) can plum tomatoes
1 teaspoon salt
1 teaspoon turmeric

1 teaspoon chili powder
Handful coriander stems, finely chopped
3 fresh green chiles, finely chopped
12 pieces chicken, mixed thighs and drumsticks, or a whole chicken, skinned, trimmed, and chopped
2 teaspoons garam masala
Handful fresh coriander leaves, chopped

1. In a frying pan (or in the crock pot if you have a sear setting), heat the oil over medium-high heat. Add the diced onions and sauté for about 5 minutes. Add the garlic and cook for an additional 10 minutes, stirring occasionally, until the onions are deeply browned and caramelized. 2. Switch the crock pot to high heat. Transfer the onion-and-garlic mixture into the crock pot. Stir in the ginger, chopped tomatoes, salt, turmeric, chili powder, coriander stems, and fresh chiles. 3. Add the chicken pieces to the crock pot, stirring to coat them with the spices and mixture. Cover and cook on low for 6 hours or on high for 4 hours, until the chicken is tender and fully cooked. 4. Once the dish is done cooking, taste for seasoning and adjust if necessary. Stir in the garam masala and fresh coriander leaves right before serving to add a burst of flavor.

Chapter 4

Beef, Pork, and Lamb

Three-bean tortilla casserole

Prep time: 30 minutes | Cook time: 8 to 10 hours | Serves 6

1 tablespoon oil
1 onion, chopped
1 green bell pepper, chopped
2 garlic cloves, minced
1 (16-ounce / 454-g) can pinto beans, drained
1 (16-ounce / 454-g) can kidney beans, drained
1 (15-ounce / 425-g) can black beans, drained
1 (4-ounce / 113-g) can

sliced black olives, drained
1 (4-ounce / 113-g) can green chilies
2 (15-ounce / 425-g) cans diced tomatoes
1 teaspoon chili powder
1 teaspoon ground cumin
6 to 8 (6-inch) flour tortillas
2 cups shredded Co-Jack cheese
Sour cream

1. Sauté onions, green peppers, and garlic in large skillet in oil. 2. Add beans, olives, chilies, tomatoes, chili powder, and cumin. 3. In greased crock pot , layer ¾ cup vegetables, a tortilla, ⅓ cup cheese. Repeat layers until all those ingredients are used, ending with sauce. 4. Cover. Cook on low 8 to 10 hours. 5. Serve with dollops of sour cream on individual servings.

Spicy cumin pork with corn

Prep time: 15 minutes | Cook time: 4 to 8 hours | Serves 6 to 8

2 tablespoons vegetable oil
1 teaspoon ground cumin
½ teaspoon chili powder
2 cloves garlic, minced
3 pounds (1.4 kg) boneless pork shoulder meat, excess fat removed, cut into 2-inch pieces
2 teaspoons salt

1 cup prepared salsa (medium, or hot if you like a bit more heat)
½ cup beef broth
1 (16-ounce / 454-g) package frozen corn, defrosted
Flour or corn tortillas for serving

1. Heat the oil in a large skillet over medium heat. Add the cumin, chili powder, and garlic and sauté until the garlic and spices are fragrant, about 1 minute. 2. Sprinkle the meat with the salt and brown the pork on all sides in the seasonings. Transfer the pork to the insert of a 5- to 7-quart crock pot . Add the salsa and broth to the skillet, scraping up any browned bits from the bottom. 3. Transfer the contents of the skillet to the insert and add the corn. Stir to combine. Cook on on high for 4 hours or low for 8 hours, until the meat is tender. Serve the pork with warmed tortillas.

Old World Sauerbraten

Prep time: 10 minutes | Cook time: 16 to 22 hours | Serves 8

1 (3½- to 4-pound / 1.6- to 1.8-kg) beef rump roast
1 cup water
1 cup vinegar
1 lemon, sliced but unpeeled
10 whole cloves

1 large onion, sliced
4 bay leaves
6 whole peppercorns
2 tablespoons salt
2 tablespoons sugar
12 gingersnaps, crumbled

1. Place the beef in a deep ceramic or glass bowl. 2. In a separate bowl, combine water, vinegar, lemon, cloves, onion, bay leaves, peppercorns, salt, and sugar. Pour this marinade over the meat. Cover the bowl and refrigerate for 24 to 36 hours, turning the meat a few times during the marinating process. 3. After marinating, place the beef in the crock pot and pour 1 cup of the marinade over the meat. 4. Cover and cook on low for 6 to 8 hours, until the meat is tender. Remove the meat from the crock pot. 5. Strain the juices from the crock pot and return the liquid to the pot. Turn the heat to high and stir in the crushed gingersnaps. Cover and cook on high for an additional 10 to 14 minutes, until the sauce has thickened. 6. Slice the beef and pour the finished sauce over the top before serving.

Fruited Beef Tagine

Prep time: 20 minutes | Cook time: 5 to 6 hours | Serves 6 to 8

1 tablespoon oil
2 pounds (907 g) beef, cut into 2-inch cubes
4 cups sliced onions
2 teaspoons ground coriander
1½ teaspoons ground cinnamon
¾ teaspoon ground ginger

1 (14½-ounce / 411-g) can beef broth, plus enough water to equal 2 cups
16 ounces (454 g) pitted prunes
Salt to taste
Fresh ground pepper to taste
Juice of one lemon

1. Heat oil in a skillet and brown the beef cubes. Once browned, transfer the beef to the crock pot and reserve the drippings in the skillet. 2. In the same skillet, sauté the onions in the drippings until they turn lightly browned. If necessary, add a little more oil to prevent sticking. Once done, transfer the onions to the crock pot with the beef. 3. Add the remaining ingredients, except for the lemon juice, to the crock pot. 4. Cover and simmer on low for 5 to 6 hours, adding the lemon juice in the final 10 minutes of cooking. 5. Serve and enjoy!

South Indian Coconut–Pork Curry

Prep time: 15 minutes | Cook time: 4 to 6 hours | Serves 6 to 8

2 pounds (907 g) boneless pork shoulder, skin removed, cut into chunks
Sea salt
Freshly ground black pepper
2 tablespoons rapeseed oil
2 teaspoons cumin seeds
1 teaspoon coriander seeds
2 onions, finely diced
5 garlic cloves, minced
1 fresh green chile, chopped

1 tablespoon freshly grated ginger
1 teaspoon ground turmeric
2 star anise
2 dried red chiles
7 to 8 ounces (198 to 227 g) canned tomatoes
1 (14-ounce / 397-g) can coconut milk
¼ pound (113 g) green beans, trimmed
Handful fresh coriander leaves, chopped

1. Season the pork generously with salt and freshly ground black pepper. 2. Heat the crock pot to high or use the sauté setting if your model has one. Add the oil to the pot, then sear the pork for 1-2 minutes on each side until browned. 3. Grind the cumin and coriander seeds in a mortar and pestle until finely ground. 4. Add the ground cumin and coriander to the crock pot, followed by the onions, garlic, green chile, ginger, turmeric, anise, and dried red chiles. Stir to combine. 5. Blend the tomatoes in a blender until smooth, then pour them into the crock pot along with the coconut milk. Stir everything together. Cover and cook on low for 6 hours, or on high for 4 hours. 6. About 30 minutes before the cooking time ends, add the trimmed green beans to the crock pot and cook for another 30 minutes. 7. Once everything is cooked through, taste and adjust the seasoning as needed. Stir in the fresh coriander leaves before serving.

Crocked Swiss Steak

Prep time: 30 minutes | Cook time: 7 hours | Serves 4

1 (1-pound / 454-g) round steak, ¾ to 1-inch thick, cubed
1 (16-ounce / 454-g) can stewed tomatoes
3 carrots, halved

lengthwise
2 potatoes, quartered
1 medium onion, quartered
Garlic powder to taste (optional)

1. Start by layering the ingredients in your crock pot, placing the meat and vegetables first. 2. Pour in any liquids or seasonings, making sure everything is evenly distributed.

3. Cover and cook on low for 7 hours, or until the meat is tender and the vegetables are just right. Keep an eye on the consistency to prevent overcooking. Serve once ready!

Cheesy chili rice casserole

Prep time: 25 minutes | Cook time: 7 hours | Serves 6

1 pound (454 g) bulk pork sausage, browned
2 cups water
1 (15½-ounce / 439-g) can chili beans
1 (14½-ounce / 411-g) can diced tomatoes
¾ cup brown rice
¼ cup chopped onions

1 tablespoon chili powder
1 teaspoon Worcestershire sauce
1 teaspoon prepared mustard
¾ teaspoon salt
⅛ teaspoon garlic powder
1 cup shredded Cheddar cheese

1. Combine all ingredients except cheese in crock pot . 2. Cover. Cook on low 7 hours. 3. Stir in cheese during last 10 minutes of cooking time.

Spicy honey–glazed Sichuan ribs

Prep time: 10 minutes | Cook time: 8 to 10 hours | Serves 6

2 teaspoons freshly ground black pepper
1 teaspoon kosher salt
½ teaspoon ground coriander
½ teaspoon garlic powder
½ teaspoon ground cumin
¼ teaspoon ground ginger
3 pounds (1.4 kg) baby back ribs, trimmed

½ cup water
1 small onion, sliced
1 garlic clove, minced
½ cup honey
½ cup Sriracha
2½ tablespoons Asian chili sauce (such as sambal oelek)
¼ cup brown sugar

1. In a small bowl, mix together the pepper, salt, coriander, garlic powder, cumin, and ginger. Rub the mix on the ribs. Add the water to the crock pot , followed by the ribs. Top the meat with the onion and garlic. Cover and cook on low for 8 to 10 hours. 2. Preheat your oven's broiler. In another small bowl, make the glaze by combining the honey, Sriracha, chili sauce, and brown sugar. Gently remove the ribs from the liquid and transfer to an aluminum foil–lined baking sheet. Discard the cooking liquid, onion, and garlic. Generously brush the ribs with the glaze and broil them, watching closely to avoid burning, until caramelized, 3 to 5 minutes. Remove them from the oven and enjoy immediately.

Korean-Style Short Ribs and Carrots

Prep time: 15 minutes | Cook time: 8 hours | Serves 2

1 tablespoon low-sodium soy sauce
1 tablespoon fish sauce
1 tablespoon rice wine vinegar
1 teaspoon Sriracha
1 teaspoon toasted sesame oil
1 teaspoon minced garlic
1 teaspoon minced fresh ginger
8 ounces (227 g) short ribs, trimmed of fat
4 carrots, cut into 2-inch pieces
2 cups low-sodium beef broth
1 scallion, white and green parts, sliced thin, for garnish

1. Start by lightly greasing the inside of the crock pot with olive oil to prevent sticking. 2. Add the onion, red pepper, parsley, and wine to the bottom of the crock pot. 3. In a small bowl, mix together the salt, black pepper, garlic, rosemary, and paprika. Rub this seasoning mixture over the lamb chops, making sure they are well-coated. For a deeper flavor, prepare this step a day ahead and let the seasoning marinate into the meat. Place the lamb chops on top of the onion and wine mixture in the crock pot, layering them as needed. 4. Arrange the potatoes on top of the lamb chops. 5. Cover and cook on low for 8 hours, allowing the flavors to meld and the meat to become tender.

Plum Sauce Pork Chops

Prep time: 20 minutes | Cook time: 3½ to 8 hours | Serves 6

¼ cup olive oil
1 teaspoon salt
½ teaspoon freshly ground black pepper
6 (1-inch-thick) pork loin chops
2 medium onions, finely chopped
1 cup plum preserves
2 tablespoons Dijon mustard
2 tablespoons fresh lemon juice
Grated zest of 1 lemon
½ cup ketchup

1. Heat the oil in a large skillet over high heat. Season the pork chops with salt and pepper, then add them to the skillet. Brown the pork chops on all sides, about 4 to 5 minutes total. 2. Once browned, transfer the pork chops to the insert of a 5- to 7-quart crock pot. Lower the heat to medium-high and add the onions to the skillet. Sauté for 3 to 5 minutes, until the onions are softened. Add the preserves to the skillet and stir to loosen any browned bits from the pan.

Transfer the onion and preserve mixture to the crock pot. 3. Stir in the mustard, lemon juice and zest, and ketchup. Mix well to combine. Cover and cook on high for 3½ to 4 hours, or on low for 6 to 8 hours. Skim off any excess fat from the sauce before serving. 4. Serve the pork chops with the sauce, keeping the crock pot set on warm to maintain the temperature.

Quick and Easy Chili

Prep time: 20 minutes | Cook time: 4 to 5 hours | Serves 4

1 pound (454 g) ground beef
1 onion, chopped
1 (16-ounce / 454-g) can stewed tomatoes
1 (11½-ounce / 326-g) can Hot V-8 juice
2 (15-ounce / 425-g) cans pinto beans
¼ teaspoon cayenne pepper
½ teaspoon salt
1 tablespoon chili powder
For Garnish:
Sour cream
Chopped green onions
Shredded cheese
Sliced ripe olives

1. Crumble the ground beef into a microwave-safe casserole dish and add the onion. Cover and microwave on high for 15 minutes. Once done, drain the excess liquid and break the meat into smaller pieces. 2. In a slow cooker, combine all the ingredients, except for the garnish items. 3. Cover and cook on low for 4 to 5 hours until the flavors are well combined. 4. Once ready, serve the dish topped with sour cream, chopped green onions, shredded cheese, and sliced ripe olives for added flavor and presentation.

North Carolina Barbecue

Prep time: 15 minutes | Cook time: 5 to 8 hours | Serves 8 to 12

1 (3- to 4-pound / 1.4- to 1.8-kg) pork loin, roast or shoulder
1 cup apple cider vinegar
¼ cup, plus 1 tablespoon, prepared mustard
¼ cup, plus 1 tablespoon, Worcestershire sauce
2 teaspoons red pepper flakes

1. Begin by removing any excess fat from the pork and placing it in the slow cooker. 2. In a separate bowl, combine the remaining ingredients, then pour the mixture over the pork. 3. Cover the slow cooker and cook on high for 5 hours or on low for 8 hours, until the meat is tender without becoming dry. 4. Once cooked, slice or shred the pork and serve it with the flavorful cooking juices drizzled on top.

Quick-and-Easy Sweet and Sour Meatballs

Prep time: 15 minutes | Cook time: 2 hours | Serves 8 to 10

2 pounds (907 g) precooked meatballs

1 cup grape jelly
2 cups cocktail sauce

1. Place the precooked meatballs in your crock pot. 2. In a medium-sized bowl, whisk together the jelly and cocktail sauce until well combined (it may still be a bit lumpy). 3. Pour the sauce mixture over the meatballs, stirring gently to coat them evenly. 4. Cover and cook on high for 1 to 2 hours, or until the sauce is fully heated and the meatballs are warm. 5. Once heated through, turn the heat to low to keep the meatballs warm until ready to serve.

Greek-Style Meatballs in Red Wine Sauce

Prep time: 30 minutes | Cook time: 3 to 8 hours | Serves 6 to 8

Sauce:
2 tablespoons extra-virgin olive oil
½ cup finely chopped onion
2 tablespoons all-purpose flour
2 cups red wine, such as Chianti, Barolo, or Zinfandel
1 cup beef broth
1 cup chicken broth
Meat Balls:
1 pound (454 g) lean ground lamb
1 pound (454 g) lean ground beef

3 cloves garlic, minced
1 cup finely chopped yellow onion
2 teaspoons dried oregano
1 teaspoon dried rosemary, crushed in the palm of your hand
2 slices bread, crusts removed, torn into pieces
¼ cup milk
2 teaspoons salt
1 teaspoon freshly ground black pepper
Grated zest of 1 lemon
½ cup finely chopped fresh parsley

1. Heat the oil in a saucepan over medium-high heat. Add the onion and sauté for 3 minutes, until softened. 2. Stir in the flour and cook, stirring, for 3 minutes. Add the wine and whisk until the mixture boils. Transfer to the insert of a 5- to 7-quart crock pot and stir in the broths. 3. Cover and keep warm while making the meatballs. 4. Combine all the meatball ingredients except the parsley in a large mixing bowl and mix until well blended. Shape into 2-inch balls and carefully place in the sauce. 5. Cover and cook on

high for 3 to 4 hours or on low for 6 to 8 hours, until the meatballs are cooked through. Skim off any fat from the top of the sauce and stir in the parsley. 6. Serve from the cooker set on warm.

Beef a la Mode

Prep time: 10 minutes | Cook time: 6 to 8 hours | Serves 6

1 (2-pound / 907-g) boneless beef roast, cut into 6 serving-size pieces
½ pound (227 g) salt pork

or bacon, cut up
3 onions, chopped
Pepper to taste
Water

1. Add the beef and pork to the slow cooker. 2. Sprinkle the onions evenly over the meat. 3. Season with pepper to taste. 4. Pour water around the meat, ensuring it's about 1 inch deep. 5. Cover and cook on low for 6 to 8 hours until the meat is tender. 6. Once cooked, serve and enjoy.

Smoky Santa Maria Tri-Tip Fajitas

Prep time: 20 minutes | Cook time: 3 to 7 hours | Serves 8

2 large onions, cut into half rounds
¼ cup firmly packed light brown sugar
2 tablespoons sweet paprika
2 teaspoons ancho chile powder
2 teaspoons garlic salt

1 teaspoon celery seeds
2 (1½- to 2-pound / 680- to 907-g) tri-tip roasts, fat trimmed, tied together with kitchen string or silicone loops
2 tablespoons olive oil
½ cup beef broth

1. Spread the onions on the bottom of the insert of a 5- to 7-quart crock pot . Combine the sugar, paprika, chile powder, garlic salt, and celery seeds in a small bowl. Rub the mixture evenly over the roasts. 2. Heat the oil in a large skillet over high heat. Add the meat and brown on all sides. 3. Transfer the meat to the slow-cooker insert. Deglaze the skillet with the broth and scrape up any browned bits from the bottom of the pan. 4. Pour the broth over the meat in the slow-cooker insert. Cover and cook on high for 3 hours or on low for 6 to 7 hours, until the meat is tender. 5. Remove the meat from the crock pot , cover with aluminum foil, and allow to rest. Remove the strings from the meat. Slice the meat thinly against the grain and serve.

Teriyaki-Glazed Sirloin with Sweet Onion Sauce

Prep time: 20 minutes | Cook time: 4 to 5 hours | Serves 6 to 8

⅔ cup soy sauce

¼ cup vegetable oil

½ cup rice wine (mirin)

¼ cup firmly packed light brown sugar

1 teaspoon freshly grated ginger

2 cloves garlic, minced

1 (2½- to 3-pound / 1.1- to 1.4-kg) sirloin roast (tri-tip or triangle sirloin works

well here)

2 cups beef broth

2 large sweet onions, such as Vidalia, coarsely chopped

2 teaspoons cornstarch mixed with 2 teaspoons of water

Chopped green onions, for garnish

Sesame seeds, for garnish

1. Combine the soy sauce, oil, rice wine, brown sugar, ginger, and garlic in a large zipper-top plastic bag. Add the sirloin to the bag, seal, and turn to coat the meat with the marinade. Refrigerate for at least 8 hours and up to 24 hours. 2. Pour the marinade and the meat into the insert of a 5- to 7-quart crock pot . Add the broth and onions. Cover and cook on high for 4 to 5 hours. 3. Remove the meat from the insert, cover with aluminum foil, and allow to rest for 15 minutes. Strain the sauce through a fine-mesh sieve into a saucepan and bring to a boil. Taste the sauce and dilute it with water or broth if it is too strong. 4. Add the cornstarch mixture and bring the sauce back to a boil, whisking constantly, until it is thickened. Keep the sauce warm on the stovetop, or transfer it to the crock pot set on warm. 5. Slice the meat and serve with the sauce, and garnish with the green onions and sesame seeds.

Meatball Party Subs

Prep time: 15 minutes | Cook time: 8 to 10 hours | Serves 30

1 (10-pound / 4.5-kg) bag prepared meatballs

1 large onion, sliced

10 good-sized fresh mushrooms, sliced

2 (26-ounce / 737-g) jars

spaghetti sauce, your choice of flavors

2 cloves garlic, minced

1 pound (454 g) Mozzarella cheese, shredded (optional)

1. Combine all ingredients except the cheese in your crock pot . Stir well to coat the meatballs with sauce. 2. Cover and cook on low 8 to 10 hours, stirring occasionally throughout cooking time to mix juices. 3. Sprinkle Mozzarella cheese and serve, if you wish.

Corned Beef Stuffing Bake

Prep time: 10 minutes | Cook time: 2 to 4 hours | Serves 4

2 cups deli-style corned beef, torn into bite-sized pieces, divided

1 (15-ounce / 425-g) can sauerkraut, drained, divided

½ cup shredded or 8 slices Swiss cheese, divided

¼ cup Thousand Island salad dressing, divided

4 cups dry packaged stuffing mix, divided

1. Spray crock pot with nonstick cooking spray. 2. Layer half of each ingredient in the order listed. 3. Repeat layers. 4. Cover and cook on low 2 to 4 hours, until casserole is cooked through and cheese has melted.

Hawaiian-Style Short Ribs

Prep time: 20 minutes | Cook time: 4 hours | Serves 6

2 red onions, cut into 1-inch wedges, root ends left intact

4 garlic cloves, smashed and peeled

1 (2-inch) piece fresh ginger, peeled and thinly sliced

4 pounds (1.8 kg) bone-in beef short ribs, cut into 3½-inch pieces

1½ cups packed dark brown sugar

1 cup low-sodium soy sauce

¼ cup plus 2 tablespoons rice vinegar

1 tablespoon hot sauce, such as Sriracha

3 cups (1-inch-cubed) pineapple

Cooked white rice, for serving

Thinly sliced scallion, for garnish

1. Start by preheating a 5- to 6-quart slow cooker. 2. Add the onions, garlic, and ginger to the slow cooker, then layer the short ribs on top in a snug, even layer. In a bowl, whisk together the brown sugar, soy sauce, vinegar, and hot sauce, then pour this mixture over the ribs. 3. Cover and cook on high for about 4 hours, or on low for 7 to 8 hours, until the ribs are nearly tender. Add the pineapple to the slow cooker and continue cooking for an additional hour on high (or 2 hours on low) until everything is tender. 4. Use a slotted spoon to transfer the ribs, pineapple, onions, and ginger to a serving platter, covering them loosely with foil. Skim the excess fat from the cooking liquid using a ladle. Serve the ribs and pineapple mixture over rice, drizzle with some of the cooking liquid, and garnish with sliced scallions. (The short ribs and cooking liquid can be stored in an airtight container in the fridge for up to 3 days.)

Dilled Pot Roast

Prep time: 5 minutes | Cook time: 7¼ to 9¼ hours | Serves 8

1 (2¾-pound / 1.3-kg) beef pot roast	¼ cup water
1 teaspoon salt	2 tablespoons wine vinegar
¼ teaspoon black pepper	4 tablespoons flour
2 teaspoons dried dill weed, divided	½ cup water
	2 cups fat-free sour cream

1. Season both sides of the beef with salt, pepper, and 1 teaspoon of dill weed. Place the beef in the crock pot. 2. Add ¼ cup of water and vinegar to the crock pot. 3. Cover and cook on low for 7 to 9 hours, until the beef is tender. 4. Once cooked, remove the beef from the pot and set aside. Turn the crock pot to high. 5. In a small bowl, mix flour with ½ cup of water until smooth. Stir this mixture into the meat drippings in the crock pot. 6. If desired, stir in the additional 1 teaspoon of dill weed. 7. Cover and cook on high for 5 minutes to thicken the sauce. 8. Stir in sour cream and mix well. 9. Cover and cook on high for another 5 minutes. 10. Slice the beef and serve with the creamy dill sauce.

Pork Loin Braised in Cider with Apples and Cream

Prep time: 20 minutes | Cook time: 4 hours | Serves 6 to 8

2 tablespoons olive oil	1 cup beef stock
½ cup Dijon mustard	4 large Gala or Braeburn apples, peeled, cored, and cut into 8 wedges each
½ cup firmly packed light brown sugar	
1 (2½- to 3-pound / 1.1- to 1.4-kg) pork loin roast, rolled and tied	¾ cup heavy cream
	Salt and freshly ground black pepper
1 large onion, finely sliced	
2 teaspoons dried thyme	1 pound (454 g) buttered cooked wide egg noodles
½ cup apple cider	

1. Heat oil in a large sauté pan over medium-high heat. In a small bowl, mix the mustard and sugar to form a paste. Spread the paste over the pork roast, coating it on all sides. Add the roast to the pan and brown it on all sides. Once browned, add the onion and thyme to the pan, cooking until the onion softens, about 3 to 5 minutes. 2. Transfer the roast, onion, and any pan drippings to the insert of a 5- to 7-quart crock pot. Pour in the cider and beef stock. Cover and cook on high for 3 hours. 3. After 3 hours, remove the lid, add the apples and cream, and cover again. Cook on high for

an additional hour. 4. Once done, remove the pork from the crock pot, cover with aluminum foil, and allow to rest for 15 minutes. Season the sauce with salt and pepper to taste. Remove the strings from the roast and slice it thinly. Serve the pork slices over buttered noodles, spooning the sauce over the meat and noodles.

Kluski Noodle and Sauerkraut Stew

Prep time: 15 minutes | Cook time: 8 to 10 hours | Serves 10

1 pound (454 g) beef stewing meat, trimmed of fat	1 envelope dry onion soup mix
1 pound (454 g) pork roast, cubed and trimmed of fat	1 (27-ounce / 765-g) can sauerkraut
2 (10¾-ounce / 305-g) cans 98% fat-free cream of mushroom soup	2 cups skim milk
	1 (12-ounce / 340-g) package kluski (or extra-sturdy) noodles

1. Combine all ingredients except noodles in crock pot. 2. Cook on low 8 to 10 hours. 3. Add uncooked noodles 2 hours before serving, or cook noodles fully, drain, and stir into chop suey 15 minutes before serving.

Italian Sausage and Peppers Stew

Prep time: 20 minutes | Cook time: 5 hours | Serves 6 to 8

2 tablespoons extra-virgin olive oil	3 medium red onions, cut into half rounds
1½ teaspoons salt	2 medium red bell peppers, seeded and sliced
½ teaspoon freshly ground black pepper	
1 tablespoon light brown sugar	2 medium yellow bell peppers, seeded and sliced
2 tablespoons tomato paste	2 medium orange bell peppers, seeded and sliced
2 medium onions, cut into half rounds	3 pounds (1.4 kg) sweet Italian sausages

1. Mix the oil, salt, pepper, sugar, and tomato paste in the insert of a 5- to 7-quart crock pot. Add the onions and bell peppers and toss to coat. 2. Add the sausages, cover, and cook on high for 5 hours, until the sausages are cooked through. Skim off any fat from the sauce. 3. Serve from the crock pot set on warm.

Apple-Braised Pork with Sauerkraut

Prep time: 7 minutes | Cook time: 4 to 5 hours | Serves 12

1 (3-pound / 1.4-kg) pork roast

3 (2-pound / 907-g) packages sauerkraut (drain and discard juice from 1 package)

2 apples, peeled and sliced

½ cup brown sugar

1 cup apple juice

1. Place meat in large crock pot . 2. Place sauerkraut on top of meat. 3. Add apples and brown sugar. Add apple juice. 4. Cover. Cook on high 4 to 5 hours. 5. Serve.

My Norwegian Meatballs

Prep time: 5 minutes | Cook time: 45 minutes | Serves 10 to 12

1 (2- to 2½-pound / 907-g to 1.1-kg) package frozen meatballs

2 or 3 (10¾-ounce / 305-g) cans cream of mushroom soup

1 (12-ounce / 340-g) can evaporated milk

1½ cups sour cream

1 cup beef broth

1 teaspoon dill weed (optional)

1. Arrange the frozen meatballs in a long, microwave-safe dish and microwave on high for 4 minutes to thaw them slightly. 2. In the meantime, mix all the remaining ingredients together in a large bowl. 3. Transfer the meatballs into the slow cooker and pour the soup mixture over them. 4. Cover and cook on high for 45 minutes, ensuring the sauce doesn't come to a boil. 5. Once done, reduce the heat to low and keep warm until it's time to serve.

Ham-Broccoli Casserole

Prep time: 20 minutes | Cook time: 4 to 5 hours | Serves 4

1 (16-ounce / 454-g) package frozen broccoli cuts, thawed and drained

2 to 3 cups cubed, cooked ham

1 (10¾-ounce / 305-g) can cream of mushroom soup

4 ounces (113 g) of your favorite mild cheese, cubed

1 cup milk

1 cup instant rice, uncooked

1 rib celery, chopped

1 small onion, chopped

1. Add the broccoli and ham to the slow cooker. 2. In a separate bowl, mix together the soup, cheese, milk, rice, celery, and onion. Stir this mixture into the broccoli and ham. 3. Cover the slow cooker and cook on low for 4 to 5 hours until the dish is heated through and the flavors have melded.

Dijon Tarragon Beef Stew

Prep time: 15 minutes | Cook time: 3½ hours | Serves 6

Salt and freshly ground black pepper

3 pounds (1.4 kg) beef sirloin, cut into 1-inch pieces

2 tablespoons olive oil

6 medium shallots, cut into half rounds

1 cup dry white wine or vermouth

½ cup Dijon mustard

1 teaspoon dried tarragon

1 cup beef broth

2 tablespoons finely chopped fresh tarragon

2 tablespoons unsalted butter

2 tablespoons all-purpose flour

1. Sprinkle 1½ teaspoons salt and ½ teaspoon pepper evenly over the meat. Heat the oil in a large skillet over high heat. Add the meat a few pieces at a time and brown. 2. Transfer the meat to the insert of a 5- to 7-quart crock pot . Add the shallots to the same skillet over medium-high heat and sauté for 1 minute, until they begin to soften. Deglaze the pan with the wine, scraping up any browned bits from the bottom of the pan, and add the mustard and dried tarragon. 3. Transfer the mixture to the crock pot and stir in the broth. Cover and cook on high for 3 hours, until the meat is tender. Skim off any fat from the top of the sauce and stir in the fresh tarragon. 4. Mix the butter and the flour together to form a paste. Add the butter mixture in pieces to the cooker. Cover and cook for an additional 30 minutes, until the sauce is thickened. 5. Season with salt and pepper before serving.

Honey BBQ Pot Roast

Prep time: 5 minutes | Cook time: 5 to 6 hours | Serves 10

1 (5-pound / 2.3-kg) roast

1 (16-ounce / 454-g) bottle honey barbecue sauce

1 small onion, chopped

1 clove garlic, minced

Black pepper (optional)

Montreal seasoning (optional)

1. Place roast in crock pot . 2. Pour barbecue sauce over top. 3. Sprinkle onion over roast, and garlic beside the roast. 4. If you wish, sprinkle with pepper and/or Montreal seasoning. 5. Cover and cook on low 5 to 6 hours. 6. Remove roast from cooker and allow to rest for 10 minutes. Slice and serve with cooking juices.

Slow-Cooked Honey BBQ Pork Chops

Prep time: 15 minutes | Cook time: 6 to 8 hours | Serves 8

8 pork chops, divided
1 large onion, sliced, divided

1 cup barbecue sauce
⅓ cup honey

1. Place one layer of pork chops in your crock pot . 2. Arrange a proportionate amount of sliced onions over top. 3. Mix barbecue sauce and honey together in a small bowl. Spoon a proportionate amount of sauce over the chops. 4. Repeat the layers. 5. Cover and cook on low 3 to 4 hours. 6. If the sauce barely covers the chops, flip them over at this point. If they're well covered, simply allow them to cook another 3 to 4 hours on low, or until they're tender but the meat is not dry.

Savory Pork Roast with Sauerkraut

Prep time: 10 minutes | Cook time: 3 to 6 hours | Serves 6

1 (2-pound / 907-g) pork roast
1 clove garlic, minced
1 medium onion, sliced

1 pint sauerkraut, or more if you wish
1 teaspoon caraway seed

1. If you have a few extra minutes, heat a nonstick skillet over medium-high heat. Once hot, place the roast in the pan and brown it on all sides for added flavor. 2. Transfer the roast, whether browned or not, into the slow cooker. 3. Add the remaining ingredients to the slow cooker in the order listed. 4. Cover and cook on high for 3 hours or on low for 4 to 6 hours, until the meat is tender but not dry.

Crocked Pulled Pork Barbecue

Prep time: 10 minutes | Cook time: 12 to 20 hours | Serves 10 to 12

2 onions, sliced
1 (4- to 5-pound / 1.8- to 2.3-kg) pork roast or fresh picnic ham
5 to 6 whole cloves

2 cups water
1 large onion, chopped
1 (16-ounce / 454-g) bottle barbecue sauce

1. Put half of sliced onions in bottom of crock pot . Add meat, cloves, and water. Cover with remaining sliced onions. 2. Cover. Cook on low 8 to 12 hours. 3. Remove bone from meat. Cut up meat. Drain liquid. 4. Return meat to crock pot . Add chopped onion and barbecue sauce. 5. Cover. Cook on high 1 to 3 hours, or on low 4 to 8 hours, stirring two or three times. 6. Serve.

Beef and Noodle Casserole

Prep time: 20 minutes | Cook time: 4 hours | Serves 10

1 pound (454 g) extra-lean ground beef
1 medium onion, chopped
1 medium green bell pepper, chopped
1 (17-ounce / 482-g) can whole-kernel corn, drained
1 (4-ounce / 113-g) can mushroom stems and pieces, drained
1 teaspoon salt

¼ teaspoon black pepper
1 (11-ounce / 312-g) jar salsa
5 cups dry medium egg noodles, cooked
1 (28-ounce / 794-g) can low-sodium diced tomatoes, undrained
1 cup low-fat shredded Cheddar cheese

1. Brown the ground beef and onion in a nonstick skillet over medium heat. Once cooked, transfer them to the slow cooker. 2. Layer the remaining ingredients on top in the order listed. 3. Cover the slow cooker and cook on low for 4 hours, allowing the flavors to meld together.

Guinness-Braised Corned Beef

Prep time: 15 minutes | Cook time: 8 to 10 hours | Serves 6 to 8

2 (12-ounce / 340-g) cans Guinness or other stout or dark ale
¼ cup firmly packed light brown sugar
2 teaspoons mustard seeds
6 whole black peppercorns

1 bay leaf
2 allspice berries
3 large sweet onions, such as Vidalia, sliced into ½-inch-thick half rounds
1 (3½- to 4-pound / 1.6- to 1.8-kg) corned beef, rinsed

1. Stir the Guinness, sugar, mustard seeds, peppercorns, bay leaf, and allspice berries together in the insert of a 5- to 7-quart crock pot . Add the onions and top with the corned beef. (Cut it in half to fit, if necessary.) 2. Cover and cook on low for 8 to 10 hours, until the meat is fork tender. Remove the meat from the cooker, cover with aluminum foil, and allow to rest for 20 minutes. 3. Remove the bay leaf, peppercorns, and allspice berries from the cooking liquid. Thinly slice the brisket across the grain to serve.

Ham with Spicy Mustard Glaze

Prep time: 20 minutes | Cook time: 3½ to 9 hours | Serves 10 to 12

1½ cups apple cider	4 whole allspice berries
1 (4-ounce / 113-g) jar Stonewall Kitchen pub mustard or other whole-grain mustard	½ cup Ruby Port
	2 (15-ounce / 425-g) cans whole berry cranberry sauce
½ cup firmly packed light brown sugar	Grated zest of 2 oranges
2 (4-inch) cinnamon sticks	½ cup orange juice
3 whole cloves	1 (5-pound / 2.3-kg) smoked ham

1. In the insert of a 5- to 7-quart slow cooker, combine the cider, mustard, sugar, and spices. Add the port, cranberry sauce, and orange zest and juice, stirring everything together. Place the ham on top of the glaze and spoon some of the glaze over the ham. 2. Cover and cook on high for 3½ to 4 hours or on low for 8 to 9 hours, occasionally spooning the glaze over the ham to keep it flavorful. 3. Once cooked, remove the ham from the slow cooker, cover with aluminum foil, and let it rest for 15 minutes. If you prefer a thicker glaze, skim off any excess fat, then strain the liquid through a fine mesh sieve into a saucepan. Bring to a boil, stirring frequently, until it reduces to about 2 cups. (Keep in mind, the ham will release some liquid, which can dilute the glaze.) 4. Slice the ham and drizzle with the reduced glaze before serving.

Give-Me-More Meatballs

Prep time: 30 minutes | Cook time: 6 to 10 hours | Serves 10

1½ cups chili sauce	beef
1 cup grape or apple jelly	1 egg
3 teaspoons brown spicy mustard	3 tablespoons dry bread crumbs
1 pound (454 g) ground	½ teaspoon salt

1. In the slow cooker, combine the chili sauce, jelly, and mustard. Stir well to mix everything together. 2. Cover the crock pot and cook on high while you prepare the meatballs. 3. In a bowl, mix the remaining ingredients and shape the mixture into 30 meatballs. Place them in a baking pan and bake at 400°F (205°C) for 15 to 20 minutes. Once done, drain the meatballs well and add them to the crock pot. Stir gently to coat the meatballs with the sauce. 4. Cover and cook on low for 6 to 10 hours, allowing the flavors to meld together.

Crocked BBQ Beef Ribs

Prep time: 5 minutes | Cook time: 8½ hours | Serves 8 to 10

1 (3- to 4-pound / 1.4- to 1.8-kg) boneless beef or short ribs	divided
	½ cup apricot or pineapple jam
1½ cups barbecue sauce,	1 tablespoon soy sauce

1. Place ribs in baking pan. 2. Combine ¾ cup barbecue sauce, jam, and soy sauce. Pour over ribs. Bake at 450°F (235°C) for 30 minutes to brown. 3. Take out of oven. Layer beef and sauce used in oven in crock pot . 4. Cover. Cook on low 8 hours. 5. Mix remaining ¾ cup barbecue sauce with sauce from crock pot . Pour over ribs and serve.

Sweet and Savory Hawaiian Sausages

Prep time: 15 minutes | Cook time: 4 to 5 hours | Serves 6 to 8

3 pounds (1.4 kg) link pork sausages	1 ripe large pineapple, peeled and cored, and cut into 1-inch chunks (about 4 cups)
2 cups pineapple juice	
3 tablespoons cornstarch	
1 teaspoon curry powder	

1. Sauté the sausages in a large skillet until browned on all sides. Transfer the sausages to the insert of a 5- to 7-quart crock pot . 2. Mix the pineapple juice, cornstarch, and curry powder in a mixing bowl, and pour into the slow-cooker insert. Add the pineapple, cover, and cook on low for 4 to 5 hours, until the sausages are cooked through and the sauce is thickened. 3. Serve from the cooker set on warm.

Cabbage and Beef Meatloaf

Prep time: 10 minutes | Cook time: 3 to 4 hours | Serves 6

1 pound (454 g) ground beef	diced
	1 tablespoon dried onion flakes
2 cups finely shredded cabbage	½ teaspoon caraway seeds
1 medium green pepper,	1 teaspoon salt

1. Combine all ingredients. Shape into loaf and place on rack in crock pot . 2. Cover. Cook on high 3 to 4 hours.

Ham and Lima Beans

Prep time: 15 minutes | Cook time: 4 to 7 hours | Serves 6

1 pound (454 g) dry lima beans

1 onion, chopped

1 bell pepper, chopped

1 teaspoon dry mustard

1 teaspoon salt

1 teaspoon pepper

½ pound (227 g) ham, finely cubed

1 cup water

1 (10¾-ounce / 305-g) can tomato soup

1. Cover the beans with water and let them soak for 8 hours. Drain well before using. 2. Combine all the ingredients in the slow cooker. 3. Cover and cook on low for 7 hours or on high for 4 hours until the beans are tender. 4. If the mixture starts to dry out during cooking, add ½ cup of water (or more if needed) and stir well. 5. Once done, serve and enjoy.

Garlic Lemon Butter Halibut

Prep time: 15 minutes | Cook time: 5 hours | Serves 6

1 cup (2 sticks) unsalted butter

½ cup olive oil

6 cloves garlic, sliced

1 teaspoon sweet paprika

½ cup lemon juice

Grated zest of 1 lemon

¼ cup finely chopped fresh chives

2 to 3 pounds (907 g to 1.4 kg) halibut fillets

½ cup finely chopped fresh Italian parsley

1. Combine the butter, oil, garlic, paprika, lemon juice, zest, and chives in the insert of a 5- to 7-quart crock pot and stir to combine. Cover and cook on low for 4 hours. 2. Add the halibut to the pot, spooning the sauce over the halibut. Cover and cook for an additional 40 minutes, until the halibut is cooked through and opaque. 3. Sprinkle the parsley evenly over the fish, and serve immediately.

Mahi-Mahi with Pineapple-Mango-Strawberry Salsa and Lentils

Prep time: 30 minutes | Cook time: 6 hours | Serves 6

1¼ cups vegetable or chicken stock

1 cup orange juice

¾ cup orange lentils

½ cup finely diced carrot

¼ cup finely diced red onion

¼ cup finely diced celery

1 tablespoon honey

6 (4- to-5-ounce / 113- to 142-g) mahi-mahi fillets

Sea salt

Black pepper

1 teaspoon lemon juice

Salsa:

¾ cup finely diced pineapple

¾ cup finely diced mango

½ cup finely diced strawberries

¼ cup finely diced red onion

2 tablespoons chopped fresh mint (or 2 teaspoons dried)

2 tablespoons orange juice

1 tablespoon lime juice

¼ teaspoon salt

1. In the slow cooker, combine the stock, orange juice, lentils, carrot, onion, celery, and honey. 2. Cover and cook on low for 5 to 5½ hours, or until the lentils are tender. 3. Lay a sheet of parchment paper over the lentils. Season the mahi-mahi lightly with salt and black pepper, then place it on the parchment (skin-side down if the skin is on). Cover again and continue cooking on low for about 25 minutes, or until the fish is opaque in the center. Once cooked, carefully lift the parchment paper with the fish and place it on a plate. 4. Stir the lemon juice into the lentils and season with salt and pepper to taste. 5. For the salsa, combine the pineapple, mango, strawberries, red onion, mint, orange juice, lime juice, and salt in a large jar. Mix well and refrigerate to allow the flavors to meld together. 6. To serve, place about ½ cup of hot lentils on a plate, top with a mahi-mahi fillet, and spoon ⅓ cup of salsa over the fish.

Delicate Lemon-Dill Poached Turbot

Prep time: 10 minutes | Cook time: 40 to 50 minutes | Serves 4

1 cup vegetable or chicken stock

½ cup dry white wine

1 yellow onion, sliced

1 lemon, sliced

4 sprigs fresh dill

½ teaspoon sea salt

4 (6-ounce / 170-g) turbot fillets

1. Combine the stock and wine in the crock pot . Cover and heat on high for 20 to 30 minutes. 2. Add the onion, lemon, dill, salt, and turbot to the crock pot . Cover and cook on high for about 20 minutes, until the turbot is opaque and cooked through according to taste. Serve hot.

Garlic Shrimp Marinara

Prep time: 15 minutes | Cook time: 6 to 7 hours | Serves 4

1 (15-ounce / 425-g) can diced tomatoes, with the juice

1 (6-ounce / 170-g) can tomato paste

1 clove garlic, minced

2 tablespoons minced fresh flat-leaf parsley

½ teaspoon dried basil

1 teaspoon dried oregano

1 teaspoon garlic powder

1½ teaspoons sea salt

¼ teaspoon black pepper

1 pound (454 g) cooked shrimp, peeled and deveined

2 cups hot cooked spaghetti or linguine, for serving

½ cup grated Parmesan cheese, for serving

1. Combine the tomatoes, tomato paste, and minced garlic in the crock pot . Sprinkle with the parsley, basil, oregano, garlic powder, salt, and pepper. 2. Cover and cook on low for 6 to 7 hours. 3. Turn up the heat to high, stir in the cooked shrimp, and cover and cook on high for about 15 minutes longer. 4. Serve hot over the cooked pasta. Top with Parmesan cheese.

Saffron Seafood Stew

Prep time: 20 minutes | Cook time: 7 hours | Serves 6 to 8

½ cup extra-virgin olive oil
2 medium onions, finely chopped
2 medium red bell peppers, seeded and finely chopped
6 cloves garlic, minced
1 teaspoon saffron threads, crushed
1 teaspoon hot paprika
1 cup finely chopped Spanish chorizo or soppressata salami
1 (28- to 32-ounce / 794- to 907-g) can crushed tomatoes
2 cups clam juice
1 cup chicken broth
2 pounds (907 g) firm-fleshed fish, such as halibut, monkfish, cod, or sea bass fillets, cut into 1-inch chunks
1½ pounds (680 g) littleneck clams
½ cup finely chopped fresh Italian parsley

1. Heat the oil in a large skillet over medium-high heat. Add the onions, bell peppers, garlic, saffron, paprika, and chorizo and sauté until the vegetables are softened, 5 to 7 minutes. Add the tomatoes and transfer the contents of the skillet to the insert of a 5- to 7-quart crock pot . Add the clam juice and broth and stir to combine. 2. Cover and cook on low for 6 hours. Add the fish and clams to the slow-cooker insert, spooning some of the sauce over the fish and pushing the clams under the sauce. 3. Cover and cook for an additional 45 to 50 minutes, until the clams have opened and the fish is cooked through and opaque. Discard any clams that haven't opened. 4. Sprinkle the parsley over the stew and serve immediately.

Creole Crayfish

Prep time: 15 minutes | Cook time: 3 to 8 hours | Serves 2

1½ cups diced celery
1 large yellow onion, chopped
2 small bell peppers, any colors, chopped
1 (8-ounce / 227-g) can tomato sauce
1 (28-ounce / 794-g) can whole tomatoes, broken up, with the juice
1 clove garlic, minced
1 teaspoon sea salt
¼ teaspoon black pepper
6 drops hot pepper sauce (like Tabasco)
1 pound (454 g) precooked crayfish meat

1. Add the celery, onion, and bell peppers to the slow cooker. Stir in the tomato sauce, tomatoes, and garlic, then season with salt, pepper, and hot sauce. 2. Cover the slow cooker and cook on high for 3 to 4 hours or on low for 6 to 8 hours, allowing the flavors to meld. 3. About 30 minutes before the cooking time is up, add the crayfish to the mixture. 4. Serve the dish hot, enjoying the rich, flavorful broth.

Pacifica Sweet-Hot Salmon

Prep time: 10 minutes | Cook time: 1½ hours | Serves 6

3 pounds (1.4 kg) salmon fillets
½ cup Colman's English mustard
¼ cup honey
2 tablespoons finely chopped fresh dill

1. Place the salmon fillets in the insert of a 5- to 7-quart slow cooker. In a small bowl, combine the mustard, honey, and dill, stirring until well mixed. 2. Pour the mustard-honey mixture evenly over the salmon. 3. Cover the slow cooker and cook on high for 1½ hours, or until the salmon is fully cooked and flakes easily with a fork. 4. Serve the salmon directly from the crock pot, spooning some of the sauce over the top.

Seafood Medley Cioppino

Prep time: 15 minutes | Cook time: 7 hours | Serves 4

Cooking oil spray
1 medium yellow onion, finely chopped
4 cloves garlic, minced
1 (15-ounce / 425-g) can diced tomatoes, with the juice
1 (10-ounce / 283-g) can diced tomatoes with green chiles
2 cups seafood stock
1 cup red wine
3 tablespoons chopped fresh basil
2 bay leaves
1 pound (454 g) cooked crab meat, shredded
1½ pounds (680 g) scallops
Sea salt
Black pepper
¼ cup fresh flat-leaf parsley, for garnish

1. Coat a large sauté pan with cooking oil spray and heat over medium-high heat. Add the onion and sauté for about 5 minutes, until softened. 2. Add the garlic and sauté until golden and fragrant, about 2 minutes. 3. Transfer the onion and garlic to the crock pot , and add the tomatoes, tomatoes with green chiles, stock, wine, basil, and bay leaves. Cover and cook on low for 6 hours. 4. About 30 minutes before the cooking time is completed, add the crab meat and scallops. Cover and cook on high for 30 minutes. The seafood will turn opaque. Season to taste with salt and pepper. Serve hot, garnished with parsley.

Fiery Mediterranean Mussels

Prep time: 15 minutes | Cook time: 7 hours | Serves 4

3 tablespoons olive oil
4 cloves garlic, minced
3 shallot cloves, minced
8 ounces (227 g) mushrooms, diced
1 (28-ounce / 794-g) can diced tomatoes, with the juice
¾ cup white wine
2 tablespoons dried oregano
½ tablespoon dried basil
½ teaspoon black pepper
1 teaspoon paprika
¼ teaspoon red pepper flakes
3 pounds (1.4 kg) mussels

1. In a large sauté pan, heat the olive oil over medium-high heat. Cook the garlic, shallots, and mushrooms for 2 to 3 minutes, until the garlic is just a bit brown and fragrant. Scrape the entire contents of the pan into the crock pot . 2. Add the tomatoes and white wine to the crock pot . Sprinkle with the oregano, basil, black pepper, paprika, and red pepper flakes. 3. Cover and cook on low for 4 to 5 hours, or on high for 2 to 3 hours. The mixture is done cooking when mushrooms are fork tender. 4. Clean and debeard the mussels. Discard any open mussels. 5. Increase the heat on the crock pot to high once the mushroom mixture is done. Add the cleaned mussels to the crock pot and secure the lid tightly. Cook for 30 more minutes. 6. To serve, ladle the mussels into bowls with plenty of broth. Discard any mussels that didn't open up during cooking. Serve hot, with crusty bread for sopping up the sauce.

Garlic Crab Claws

Prep time: 10 minutes | Cook time: 5½ hours | Serves 6 to 8

1 cup (2 sticks) unsalted butter
½ cup olive oil
10 cloves garlic, sliced
2 tablespoons Old Bay seasoning
2 cups dry white wine or vermouth
1 lemon, thinly sliced
3 to 4 pounds (1.4 to 1.8 kg) cooked crab legs and claws, cracked

1. In the insert of a 5- to 7-quart slow cooker, combine the butter, oil, garlic, seasoning, wine, and lemon. 2. Cover and cook on low for 4 hours, allowing the flavors to meld. Add the crab, spoon the sauce over it, and cook for an additional 1½ hours, turning the crab occasionally in the sauce to ensure even flavor. 3. Once ready, serve the crab directly from the slow cooker, keeping it set on warm.

Shrimp and Artichoke Barley Risotto

Prep time: 15 minutes | Cook time: 3 hours | Serves 4

3 cups seafood stock (or chicken stock)
1 teaspoon olive oil
1 yellow onion, chopped
3 cloves garlic, minced
1 (9-ounce / 255-g) package frozen artichoke hearts, thawed and quartered
1 cup uncooked pearl barley
Black pepper
1 pound (454 g) shrimp, peeled and deveined
2 ounces (57 g) Parmesan or Pecorino Romano cheese, grated
2 teaspoons lemon zest
4 ounces (113 g) fresh baby spinach

1. Bring the seafood stock to a boil in a medium saucepan. Once boiling, remove from heat and set aside. 2. In a nonstick skillet over medium-high heat, heat the olive oil. Add the onion and sauté until softened, about 5 minutes. Add the garlic and sauté for an additional 1 minute. 3. Transfer the sautéed onion and garlic to the slow cooker. Add the artichoke hearts and barley, then season with pepper. Pour in the seafood stock and stir everything together. 4. Cover the slow cooker and cook on high for 3 hours, or until the barley is tender and the liquid has mostly been absorbed. 5. About 15 minutes before the cooking time is complete, stir in the shrimp and grated cheese. Cover and continue cooking on high for another 10 minutes, or until the shrimp turn opaque. 6. Stir in the lemon zest and fold in the baby spinach, cooking for about 1 minute until wilted. 7. Serve the risotto in individual bowls while hot.

Garlic Herb Tilapia Packets

Prep time: 5 minutes | Cook time: 2 hours | Serves 4

2 tablespoons butter, at room temperature
2 cloves garlic, minced
2 teaspoons minced fresh flat-leaf parsley
4 tilapia fillets
Sea salt
Black pepper

1. In a small bowl, mix the butter, garlic, and parsley to combine. 2. Pull out a large sheet of aluminum foil and put it on the counter. Place the fillets in the middle of the foil. 3. Season the fish generously with salt and pepper. 4. Evenly divide the butter mixture among the fillets and place on top. 5. Wrap the foil around the fish, sealing all sides and crimping the edges to make a packet. Place in the crock pot , cover, and cook on high for 2 hours. Serve hot.

Lemon-Dijon Salmon with Dill Barley

Prep time: 15 minutes | Cook time: 2 hours | Serves 6

1 medium yellow onion, diced
2 teaspoons garlic, minced
2 teaspoons olive oil
2 cups vegetable or chicken stock
1 cup quick-cooking barley
1 tablespoon minced fresh dill weed
1½ pounds (680 g) salmon

fillets
Sea salt
Black pepper
Lemon-Dijon Sauce:
⅓ cup Dijon mustard
3 tablespoons olive oil
3 tablespoons fresh lemon juice
⅓ cup plain Greek yogurt
1 clove garlic, minced

1. In a microwave-safe bowl, combine the onion, garlic, and oil. Heat on 70% power for 4 to 5 minutes, stirring occasionally. Once softened, transfer the mixture to the slow cooker. 2. Add the stock, barley, and dill weed to the slow cooker and stir everything together. 3. Season the salmon fillets with salt and pepper, then gently place them on top of the barley mixture. 4. Cover the slow cooker and cook on low for about 2 hours, until the salmon is cooked through and the barley is tender. 5. For the Lemon-Dijon Sauce: In a small bowl, whisk together Dijon mustard, olive oil, lemon juice, Greek yogurt, and garlic. Set aside to allow the flavors to meld. 6. To serve, spoon some barley onto a plate, top with a salmon fillet, and drizzle with the Lemon-Dijon sauce.

Miso-Glazed Black Cod

Prep time: 15 minutes | Cook time: 5 hours | Serves 6

½ cup white miso paste
¼ cup rice wine (mirin)
¼ firmly packed light brown sugar
1 teaspoon rice vinegar
1 ½ cups water
2 pounds (907 g) black cod (if unavailable, use fresh

cod, halibut, sea bass, or salmon)
6 green onions, finely chopped, using the white and tender green parts
¼ cup toasted sesame seeds for garnish

1. Combine the miso, rice wine, sugar, rice vinegar, and water in the insert of a 5- to 7-quart crock pot . 2. Cover and cook on low for 4 hours. Add the cod, spooning the sauce over the top. Cover and cook for an additional 30 to 45 minutes. 3. Remove the cod from the slow-cooker insert and cover with aluminum foil to keep warm. Pour

the sauce in a saucepan. Bring to a boil and reduce by half until it begins to look syrupy, about 15 to 20 minutes. Add the green onions to the sauce. 4. Serve each piece of cod in a pool of the sauce, and sprinkle each serving with sesame seeds. Serve any additional sauce on the side.

Poached Salmon Provenç

Prep time: 15 minutes | Cook time: 1½ to 2 hours | Serves 6

3 pounds (1.4 kg) salmon fillets
½ cup dry white wine or vermouth
4 cloves garlic, peeled
1½ teaspoons finely chopped fresh rosemary
2 teaspoons finely chopped fresh thyme leaves

2 teaspoons finely chopped fresh tarragon
½ cup olive oil
1 (28- to 32-ounce / 794- to 907-g) can plum tomatoes, drained
½ cup heavy cream
Salt and freshly ground black pepper

1. Place the salmon in the insert of a 5- to 7-quart slow cooker and pour in the white wine. 2. In a food processor, combine the garlic, rosemary, thyme, tarragon, oil, and tomatoes. Process until smooth, then spoon the mixture over the salmon in the slow cooker. 3. Cover and cook on high for 1½ to 2 hours, or until the salmon is cooked through. 4. Carefully transfer the salmon to a serving platter and remove the skin. Pour the sauce into a saucepan and bring to a boil, reducing it by about ¼ cup. Stir in the heavy cream and season with salt and pepper to taste. 5. Serve the salmon topped with the creamy sauce.

Cumin Lime Halibut

Prep time: 10 minutes | Cook time: 3½ hours | Serves 6

3 cups prepared medium-hot salsa
2 tablespoons fresh lime juice
1 teaspoon ground cumin
2 to 3 pounds (907 g to 1.4

kg) halibut fillets
1½ cup finely shredded Monterey Jack cheese (or Pepper Jack for a spicy topping)

1. Combine the salsa, lime juice, and cumin in the insert of a 5- to 7-quart crock pot and stir. Cover the crock pot and cook on low for 2 hours. 2. Put the halibut in the cooker and spoon some of the sauce over the top of the fish. Sprinkle the cheese evenly over the fish. Cover and cook for an additional 30 to 45 minutes. 3. Remove the halibut from the crock pot and serve on a bed of the sauce.

Cajun Lemon-Butter Shrimp

Prep time: 15 minutes | Cook time: 4 hours | Serves 6 to 8

1 cup (2 sticks) unsalted butter
¼ cup olive oil
8 cloves garlic, sliced
2 teaspoons dried oregano
1 teaspoon dried thyme
½ teaspoon freshly ground black pepper
Pinch of cayenne pepper
2 teaspoons sweet paprika
¼ cup Worcestershire sauce
¼ cup lemon juice
3 pounds (1.4 kg) large shrimp, peeled and deveined
½ cup finely chopped fresh Italian parsley

1. Put the butter, oil, garlic, oregano, thyme, pepper, cayenne, paprika, Worcestershire, and lemon juice in the insert of a 5- to 7-quart crock pot . Cover and cook on low for 4 hours. 2. Turn the cooker up to high and add the shrimp, tossing them in the butter sauce. Cover and cook for an additional 10 to 5 minutes, until the shrimp are pink. 3. Transfer the shrimp from the crock pot to a large serving bowl and pour the sauce over the shrimp. Sprinkle with the parsley and serve.

Moroccan Sea Bass

Prep time: 20 minutes | Cook time: 3 to 4 hours | Serves 8

2 tablespoons extra-virgin olive oil
1 large yellow onion, finely chopped
1 medium red bell pepper, cut into ½-inch strips
1 medium yellow bell pepper, cut into ½-inch strips
4 garlic cloves, minced
1 teaspoon saffron threads, crushed in the palm of your hand
1½ teaspoons sweet paprika
¼ teaspoon hot paprika or ¼ teaspoon smoked
paprika (or pimentón)
½ teaspoon ground ginger
1 (15-ounce / 425-g) can diced tomatoes, with the juice
¼ cup fresh orange juice
2 pounds (907 g) fresh sea bass fillets
¼ cup finely chopped fresh flat-leaf parsley
¼ cup finely chopped fresh cilantro
Sea salt
Black pepper
1 navel orange, thinly sliced, for garnish

1. In a large skillet, heat olive oil over medium-high heat. Add the onion, red and yellow bell peppers, garlic, saffron, sweet paprika, hot or smoked paprika, and ginger. Cook, stirring often, for about 3 minutes, or until the onion begins to soften. 2. Stir in the tomatoes and cook for an additional 2 minutes to let the flavors combine. 3. Transfer the mixture to the slow cooker and stir in the orange juice. 4. Lay the sea bass fillets on top of the tomato mixture, then spoon some of the mixture over the fish. Cover and cook on high for 2 hours, or on low for 3 to 4 hours, until the sea bass is opaque in the center. 5. Carefully remove the fish from the slow cooker with a spatula and transfer to a serving platter. Cover loosely with aluminum foil to keep warm. 6. Skim off any excess fat from the sauce, then stir in the parsley and cilantro. Season with salt and pepper to taste. 7. Spoon some of the sauce over the fish and garnish with orange slices. Serve hot, with the remaining sauce on the side for passing.

Seafood Stew

Prep time: 15 minutes | Cook time: 6 hours | Serves 8

1 pound (454 g) waxy baby potatoes, such as Yukon Gold
2 medium onions, finely chopped
2 celery stalks, finely chopped
5 garlic cloves, minced
1 (28-ounce / 794-g) can crushed tomatoes
1 (8-ounce / 227-g) bottle clam juice
8 ounces (227 g) low-sodium fish stock
1 (6-ounce / 170-g) can tomato paste
1 tablespoon balsamic vinegar
1 teaspoon sugar
½ teaspoon celery salt
½ teaspoon kosher salt, plus more for seasoning
½ teaspoon freshly ground black pepper, plus more for seasoning
2 bay leaves
1 pound (454 g) firm-fleshed white fish, such as cod, cut into 1-inch pieces
½ pound (227 g) medium uncooked shrimp, shelled and deveined
½ pound (227 g) scallops, small side muscle removed, halved
¼ cup finely chopped flat-leaf parsley, for garnish

1. In the slow cooker, combine the potatoes, onions, celery, garlic, tomatoes, clam juice, fish stock, tomato paste, vinegar, sugar, celery salt, kosher salt, pepper, and bay leaves. Stir well to mix. Cover and cook on low for 6 hours, or until the potatoes are tender when pierced with a fork. 2. About 30 minutes before serving, add the white fish, shrimp, and scallops to the slow cooker. Cover and continue cooking on low until the seafood is cooked through. 3. Remove and discard the bay leaves. Taste and adjust seasoning with additional salt and pepper, if necessary. 4. Ladle the stew into bowls, garnish with fresh parsley, and serve hot.

Cajun Creole Shrimp and Sausage Stew

Prep time: 15 minutes | Cook time: 3½ to 7 hours | Serves 6

¾ pound (340 g) andouille sausage, cut into ½-inch rounds (you may substitute Kiel-basa if you cannot find andouille sausage)
1 red onion, sliced into wedges
2 garlic cloves, minced
2 celery stalks, coarsely chopped
1 red or green bell pepper, coarsely chopped
2 tablespoons all-purpose flour
1 (28-ounce / 794-g) can diced tomatoes, with their juice
¼ teaspoon cayenne pepper
Coarse sea salt
½ pound (227 g) large shrimp, peeled and deveined
2 cups fresh okra, sliced (you may substitute frozen and thawed, if necessary)

1. Put the sausage, onion, garlic, celery, and bell pepper into the crock pot . Sprinkle with the flour and toss to coat. 2. Add the tomatoes and ½ cup water. Sprinkle with the cayenne pepper and season with salt. 3. Cover and cook on high for 3½ hours or on low for 7 hours, until the vegetables are tender. 4. Add the shrimp and okra. Cover and cook until the shrimp are opaque throughout, on high for 30 minutes or on low for 1 hour. Serve hot.

Spicy Barbecued Scallops and Shrimp

Prep time: 20 minutes | Cook time: 1 hour | Serves 2

½ teaspoon paprika
½ teaspoon garlic powder
¼ teaspoon onion powder
¼ teaspoon cayenne pepper
¼ teaspoon dried oregano
¼ teaspoon dried thyme
½ teaspoon sea salt
½ teaspoon black pepper
2 cloves garlic, minced
½ cup olive oil
¼ cup Worcestershire sauce
1 tablespoon hot pepper sauce (like Tabasco)
Juice of 1 lemon
1 pound (454 g) scallops
1 pound (454 g) large shrimp, unpeeled
1 green onion, finely chopped

1. In a small bowl, combine the paprika, garlic powder, onion powder, cayenne pepper, oregano, thyme, ½ teaspoon salt, and ¼ teaspoon black pepper. 2. Add the paprika blend, garlic, olive oil, Worcestershire sauce, hot pepper sauce, and lemon juice to the slow cooker. Season with additional salt and pepper to taste. 3. Cover and cook on high for 30 minutes, or until the sauce is hot and well combined. 4. Rinse the scallops and shrimp, then drain thoroughly. 5. Spoon half of the sauce from the slow cooker into a glass measuring cup. 6. Place the scallops and shrimp in the slow cooker with the remaining sauce, then drizzle with the sauce from the measuring cup. Stir gently to coat the seafood. 7. Cover and cook on high for an additional 30 minutes, or until the scallops and shrimp are opaque. 8. Switch the slow cooker to the "warm" setting and serve. Garnish with chopped green onions before serving.

Moroccan Style Lemon Saffron Sea Bass

Prep time: 25 minutes | Cook time: 6 to 7½ hours | Serves 6

2 pounds (907 g) sea bass fillets
½ cup olive oil
Grated zest of 1 lemon
¼ cup lemon juice
1 teaspoon sweet paprika
½ cup finely chopped fresh cilantro
2 cloves garlic, chopped
1 medium onion, finely chopped
1 teaspoon ground cumin
½ teaspoon saffron threads, crushed
1 (28- to 32-ounce / 794- to 907-g) can crushed tomatoes, with their juice
6 medium Yukon gold potatoes, quartered
1 teaspoon salt
½ teaspoon freshly ground black pepper
½ cup finely chopped fresh Italian parsley

1. Place the fish in a zipper-top plastic bag. 2. Whisk ¼ cup of the oil, the zest, lemon juice, paprika, and cilantro together in a small bowl. Pour the marinade over the fish in the bag. Seal the bag and refrigerate for at least 1 hour or up to 4 hours. 3. Heat the remaining ¼ cup oil in a large skillet over medium-high heat. Add the garlic, onion, cumin, and saffron and sauté until the onion is softened, 5 to 7 minutes. 4. Add the tomatoes and stir to combine. Place the potatoes in the bottom of the insert of a 5- to 7-quart crock pot and sprinkle them evenly with the salt and pepper, tossing to coat. Add the tomato mixture to the insert. Cover and cook on low for 5 to 6 hours, until the potatoes are almost tender. 5. Pour the marinade into the insert and stir the potatoes and sauce to combine. Put the fish on top of the potatoes and spoon some of the sauce over the top. Cook for an additional 1 to 1½ hours, until the sea bass is cooked through and is opaque in the center. 6. Sprinkle the parsley evenly over the top of the sea bass and serve immediately, scooping up some potatoes and sauce with the fish.

Beantown Scallops

Prep time: 10 minutes | Cook time: 4½ hours | Serves 6

1 cup (2 sticks) unsalted butter	¼ cup dry sherry
2 tablespoons olive oil	2 pounds (907 g) dry-pack sea scallops
2 cloves garlic, minced	½ cup finely chopped fresh Italian parsley
2 teaspoons sweet paprika	

1. Place the butter, oil, garlic, paprika, and sherry in the insert of a 5- to 7-quart slow cooker. 2. Cover and cook on low for 4 hours. Once done, switch the cooker to high and add the scallops, tossing them gently in the butter sauce. Cover and cook on high for 30 to 40 minutes, or until the scallops are opaque. 3. Carefully transfer the scallops and sauce to a serving platter. Garnish with parsley and serve hot.

Bouillabaisse

Prep time: 25 minutes | Cook time: 7 to 9 hours | Serves 6 to 8

¼ cup extra-virgin olive oil	to 907-g) can crushed tomatoes, with their juice
3 leeks, cleaned and coarsely chopped, using the white and tender green parts	½ cup white wine or dry vermouth
4 cloves garlic, sliced	3 cups clam juice
1 bulb fennel, ends trimmed, coarsely chopped	1 cup chicken broth
Grated zest of 1 orange	½ pound (227 g) littleneck clams
1 teaspoon dried thyme	½ pound (227 g) mussels
1 teaspoon saffron threads, crushed	3 pounds (1.4 kg) thick-fleshed fish, cut into 1-inch chunks
Pinch of cayenne pepper	½ cup finely chopped fresh Italian parsley
1 (28- to 32-ounce / 794-	

1. Begin by heating the oil in a large pan over medium-high heat. Add the leeks, garlic, fennel, zest, thyme, saffron, and cayenne, sautéing until the vegetables soften, about 2 minutes. Next, pour in the tomatoes and wine, cooking for 10 minutes to allow the flavors to concentrate. Once done, transfer this mixture to your slow cooker insert. 2. Pour the clam juice and broth into the slow cooker, stirring well to combine. Cover and let it cook on low for 6 to 8 hours. After this time, remove the lid and carefully add the clams and mussels to the sauce. 3. Gently place the fish fillets on top of the shellfish, spooning some of the sauce over the fish. Cover the crock pot again and cook on high for 45 minutes, or until the fish is tender and opaque, and the shellfish have opened. 4. Discard any clams or mussels that remain closed. Sprinkle chopped parsley over the dish before serving it hot.

Bayou Gulf Shrimp Gumbo

Prep time: 35 minutes | Cook time: 5 hours | Serves 6

½ pound (227 g) bacon strips, chopped	2 tablespoons Worcestershire sauce
3 celery ribs, chopped	1 teaspoon kosher salt
1 medium onion, chopped	1 teaspoon dried marjoram
1 medium green pepper, chopped	2 pounds (907 g) uncooked large shrimp, peeled and deveined
2 garlic cloves, minced	
2 (8-ounce / 227-g) bottles clam juice	2½ cups frozen sliced okra, thawed
1 (14½-ounce / 411-g) can diced tomatoes, undrained	Hot cooked rice

1. In a large skillet, cook the bacon over medium heat until crisp. Remove the bacon with a slotted spoon and drain on paper towels, reserving 2 tablespoons of the drippings. In the same skillet, sauté the celery, onion, green pepper, and garlic in the reserved drippings until tender. 2. Transfer the sautéed mixture to a 4-quart slow cooker. Stir in the bacon, clam juice, tomatoes, Worcestershire sauce, salt, and marjoram. Cover and cook on low for 4 hours. 3. Add the shrimp and okra to the slow cooker. Cover and cook for an additional hour, or until the shrimp are pink and the okra is heated through. Serve hot over rice.

Honeyed Salmon

Prep time: 10 minutes | Cook time: 1 hour | Serves 6

6 (6-ounce / 170-g) salmon fillets	Worcestershire sauce
½ cup honey	1 tablespoon water
2 tablespoons lime juice	2 cloves garlic, minced
3 tablespoons	1 teaspoon ground ginger
	½ teaspoon black pepper

1. Start by placing the salmon fillets into the crock pot. 2. In a medium bowl, whisk together the honey, lime juice, Worcestershire sauce, water, garlic, ginger, and pepper until fully combined. Pour this sauce over the salmon fillets. 3. Cover the crock pot and cook on high for 1 hour, until the salmon is fully cooked and flaking easily with a fork.

Rosemary Parmesan Cod

Prep time: 20 minutes | Cook time: 1 hour | Serves 6

6 tablespoons olive oil
3 tablespoons all-purpose flour
1½ teaspoons sea salt
½ tablespoon dry mustard
1 teaspoon rosemary
¼ tablespoon ground nutmeg
1¼ cups milk
2 teaspoons lemon juice
⅓ cup grated Parmesan cheese
⅓ cup grated Asiago cheese
⅓ cup grated Romano cheese
3 pounds (1.4 kg) Pacific cod fillets

Make the Orange Layer: 1. Heat the olive oil in a small saucepan over medium heat. Stir in the flour, salt, mustard, rosemary, and nutmeg. 2. Gradually add the milk, stirring constantly until thickened. 3. Add the lemon juice, and the Parmesan, Asiago, and Romano cheeses to the saucepan. Stir until the cheeses are melted. 4. Place the fish into the crock pot , and spoon the cheese sauce over the fish. Cover and cook on high for 1 to 1½ hours or until the fish flakes. Serve hot.

Smoked Salmon and Potato Casserole

Prep time: 10 minutes | Cook time: 8 hours | Serves 2

1 teaspoon butter, at room temperature, or extra-virgin olive oil
2 eggs
1 cup 2% milk
1 teaspoon dried dill
⅛ teaspoon sea salt
Freshly ground black pepper
2 medium russet potatoes, peeled and sliced thin
4 ounces (113 g) smoked salmon

1. Start by greasing the inside of the slow cooker with butter to prevent sticking. 2. In a separate bowl, whisk together the eggs, milk, dill, salt, and a few grinds of black pepper until well combined. 3. Layer one-third of the sliced potatoes at the bottom of the crock pot, then top with one-third of the salmon. Pour one-third of the egg mixture over the salmon. Repeat the layers, alternating between potatoes, salmon, and egg mixture until everything is used. 4. Cover the slow cooker and cook on low for 8 hours, or you can leave it to cook overnight for a delicious, hearty breakfast.

Miso Honey Poached Salmon

Prep time: 10 minutes | Cook time: 1½ hours | Serves 8

3 pounds (1.4 kg) salmon fillets
3 tablespoons white miso
3 tablespoons honey
¼ cup rice wine (mirin) or dry sherry
2 teaspoons freshly grated ginger

1. place the salmon in the insert of a 5- to 7-quart crock pot . 2. Combine the miso, honey, rice wine, and ginger in a mixing bowl and stir. 3. Pour the sauce over the salmon in the crock pot . Cover and cook on high for 1½ hours, until the salmon is cooked through and registers 165°F (74°C) on an instant-read thermometer inserted in the center of a thick fillet. 4. Carefully remove the salmon from the slow-cooker insert with a large spatula. Remove the skin from the underside of the salmon (if necessary) and arrange the salmon on a serving platter. 5. Strain the sauce through a fine-mesh sieve into a saucepan. Boil the sauce, reduce it to a syrupy consistency, and serve with the salmon.

Slow-Cooked Olive Oil Tuna

Prep time: 5 minutes | Cook time: 3 to 4 hours | Serves 6

3 pounds (1.4 kg) tuna fillets
Olive oil to cover the fish
1 teaspoon coarse sea salt

1. Place the tuna in the insert of a 5- to 7-quart crock pot and pour the oil over the tuna. The oil should cover the tuna, and depending on the shape of your crock pot , you may need to add a bit more oil. Add the salt to the slow-cooker insert. 2. Cover and cook on low for 3 to 4 hours, until the tuna is cooked through and is white. Remove the tuna from the oil and cool completely before using.

Chapter 6
Beans and Grains

Herbed Swiss Lentils and Rice

Prep time: 10 minutes | Cook time: 6 to 8 hours | Serves 4

2¾ cups reduced-sodium fat-free chicken broth
¾ cup water
¾ cup dry lentils, rinsed
¾ cup onions, chopped
½ cup dry wild rice
½ teaspoon dried basil
¼ teaspoon dried oregano

¼ teaspoon dried thyme
⅛ teaspoon garlic powder
½ teaspoon salt
¼ teaspoon black pepper
1 cup shredded reduced-fat Swiss cheese
Fat-free cooking spray

1. Spray crock pot with fat-free cooking spray. 2. Combine all ingredients except cheese in crock pot . 3. Cook on low 6 to 8 hours, or until lentils and rice are tender. Do not remove lid until it has cooked at least 6 hours. 4. Stir in shredded cheese 5 to 10 minutes before serving.

Broccoli-Rice Casserole

Prep time: 5 minutes | Cook time: 3 to 4 hours | Serves 6

1 cup minute rice, uncooked
1 (1-pound / 454-g) package frozen chopped broccoli

1 (8-ounce / 227-g) jar processed cheese spread
1 (10¾-ounce / 305-g) can cream of mushroom soup

1. Combine all ingredients in the crock pot, stirring well to ensure everything is evenly mixed. 2. Cover and cook on high for 3 to 4 hours, checking occasionally, until the rice and broccoli are tender but still holding their shape, avoiding any overcooking or dryness.

Couscous and Raisin Wheat Berries

Prep time: 10 minutes | Cook time: 2 hours | Serves 4 to 6

1 cup wheat berries
1 cup couscous or small pasta like orzo
1 (14½-ounce / 411-g) can

broth
½ to 1 broth can of water
½ cup dried raisins

1. Cover wheat berries with water and soak 2 hours before cooking. Drain. Spoon wheat berries into crock pot . 2. Combine with remaining ingredients in crock pot . 3. Cover. Cook on low until liquid is absorbed and berries are soft, about 2 hours.

Tuscan Garlic Garbanzo Beans

Prep time: 15 minutes | Cook time: 6 to 7 hours | Serves 6 to 8

2 tablespoons extra-virgin olive oil
3 cloves garlic, minced
1 medium onion, finely chopped
2 teaspoons fresh rosemary leaves, finely chopped
2 (14- to 15-ounce / 397- to 425-g) cans crushed tomatoes

2 tablespoons dry red wine
4 (14- to 15-ounce / 397- to 425-g) cans garbanzo beans, rinsed and drained
1½ teaspoons salt
½ teaspoon freshly ground black pepper
½ cup finely chopped fresh Italian parsley

1. Heat the oil in a medium skillet over medium-high heat. Add the garlic, onion, and rosemary and sauté until the onion is softened, about 3 minutes. Add the tomatoes and wine and swirl in the pan to combine. 2. Transfer the contents of the skillet to the insert of a 5- to 7-quart crock pot and stir in the beans along with the salt and pepper. Cover and cook on low for 6 to 7 hours, until the beans are soft and creamy. 3. Stir in the parsley and serve.

Creamy Gorgonzola Risotto

Prep time: 10 minutes | Cook time: 2½ hours | Serves 4 to 6

½ cup (1 stick) unsalted butter
2 tablespoons olive oil
½ cup finely chopped shallots (about 4 medium)
1½ cups Arborio or

Carnaroli rice
¼ cup dry white wine or vermouth
4 cups chicken broth
1 cup crumbled Gorgonzola cheese

1. Coat the insert of a 5- to 7-quart crock pot with nonstick cooking spray or line it with a slow-cooker liner according to the manufacturer's directions. 2. Heat ¼ cup of the butter with the oil in a large saucepan over medium-high heat. Add the shallots and sauté until softened, about 4 minutes. Add the rice and cook, stirring to coat with the butter, until the rice begins to look opaque. Add the wine and cook until the wine evaporates. 3. Transfer the mixture to the slow-cooker insert and stir in the broth. Cover and cook on high for 2½ hours; check the risotto at 2 hours to make sure that the broth hasn't evaporated. 4. Stir in the remaining butter and Gorgonzola before serving immediately.

Herbed Bulgur with Tomato and Mint

Prep time: 15 minutes | Cook time: 5 to 6 hours | Serves 8

2 cups medium bulgur
2 tablespoons extra-virgin olive oil
1 medium onion, finely chopped
3 cloves garlic, minced
Pinch of red pepper flakes
1 (14- to 15-ounce / 397- to 425-g) can chopped

tomatoes, drained but juice reserved
3½ cups chicken or vegetable broth
1 teaspoon salt
¼ cup finely chopped fresh basil
¼ cup finely chopped fresh mint

1. Coat the insert of a 5- to 7-quart crock pot with nonstick cooking spray and add the bulgur. Heat the oil in a large skillet over medium-high heat. Add the onion, garlic, and red pepper flakes and sauté until the onion is softened, about 3 minutes. Add the drained tomatoes and cook until there is no liquid left in the pan. 2. Pour the broth in the skillet and scrape up any browned bits on the bottom of the pan. Transfer the contents of the skillet to the slow-cooker insert and stir in the reserved tomato juice and the salt. Cover and cook on low for 5 to 6 hours, until the bulgur is tender and the liquid is absorbed. 3. Stir in the basil and mint and serve from the cooker set on warm.

Five Baked Beans

Prep time: 10 minutes | Cook time: 4 to 12 hours | Serves 12

6 slices turkey bacon
1 cup onions, chopped
1 clove garlic, minced
1 (16-ounce / 454-g) can low-sodium lima beans, drained
1 (16-ounce / 454-g) can low-sodium beans with tomato sauce, undrained
1 (15½-ounce / 439-g) can low-sodium red kidney beans, drained
1 (15-ounce / 425-g) can low-sodium butter beans,

drained
1 (15-ounce / 425-g) can low-sodium garbanzo beans, drained
¾ cup ketchup
½ cup unsulphured molasses
¼ cup brown sugar
1 tablespoon prepared mustard
1 tablespoon Worcestershire sauce
1 onion sliced and cut into rings (optional)

1. In a nonstick skillet, fry the bacon until crispy and browned. 2. In the crock pot, combine the chopped onions, crispy bacon, garlic, lima beans, beans with tomato sauce,

kidney beans, butter beans, garbanzo beans, ketchup, molasses, brown sugar, mustard, and Worcestershire sauce. Stir everything well. 3. If desired, add extra onions on top for added flavor. 4. Cover and cook on low for 10 to 12 hours, or on high for 4 to 5 hours, until everything is well-cooked and flavorful.

Asparagus Risotto

Prep time: 15 minutes | Cook time: 5½ hours | Serves 2

Nonstick cooking spray
1½ cups Arborio rice
1 leek, white and light green parts only, sliced
2 garlic cloves, minced
¼ cup dry white wine
4 cups vegetable broth

½ teaspoon salt
⅛ teaspoon freshly ground black pepper
½ pound (227 g) asparagus
½ cup grated Parmesan cheese
1 tablespoon butter

1. Coat the crock pot insert with nonstick cooking spray. 2. In the crock pot, combine the rice, leek, garlic, wine, broth, salt, and pepper, mixing everything together. 3. Cover and cook on low for 5 hours, or until the rice is fully tender. Stir to ensure it's evenly cooked. 4. While the rice cooks, wash and trim the asparagus, cutting it into 1-inch pieces. 5. Once the rice is done, add the asparagus to the crock pot, cover, and cook on high for 30 minutes, or until the asparagus is tender but still crisp. 6. Stir in the cheese and butter, then cover and let the dish sit for 5 minutes before serving.

Cheesy Grits Casserole

Prep time: 10 minutes | Cook time: 8 hours | Serves 8

1 cup stone-ground grits
4½ cups chicken broth
4 tablespoons (½ stick) unsalted butter, melted and slightly cooled

2 large eggs, beaten
½ cup heavy cream
2 cup finely shredded mild Cheddar cheese

1. Lightly grease the crock pot insert with nonstick spray or use a slow-cooker liner according to the manufacturer's instructions. 2. Add the grits, broth, and butter to the slow-cooker insert, stirring to combine. Cover and cook on low for 4 hours. Once the grits are cooked, stir in the eggs, cream, and cheese. Cover and cook for an additional 4 hours, or until the grits are smooth and creamy and the cheese has fully melted. 3. Keep the dish warm in the cooker and serve directly from it.

Colonial Williamsburg Spoon Bread

Prep time: 10 minutes | Cook time: 3½ hours | Serves 8

3 cups cornmeal
3 cups water
3 cups milk
⅓ cup sugar
2 tablespoons baking

powder
½ cup (1 stick) unsalted butter, melted and cooled slightly
8 large eggs

1. Lightly grease the insert of a 5- to 7-quart crock pot with nonstick cooking spray. 2. In a large mixing bowl, combine the cornmeal, water, and milk, stirring for 3 to 5 minutes to create a smooth base. Add the sugar, baking powder, butter, and eggs, and mix with a wooden spoon until the batter is smooth and well combined. Transfer the mixture to the crock pot insert. 3. Cover and cook on high for 3 hours, or until the top is firm. After 3 hours, uncover and cook for an additional 30 minutes to finish setting the top. 4. Serve the spoon bread directly from the crock pot, keeping it on the warm setting.

Sweet and Savory Bean Medley

Prep time: 15 minutes | Cook time: 3 to 4 hours | Serves 6 to 8

1 pound (454 g) ground beef, browned and drained
1 (14¾-ounce / 418-g) can lima beans
1 (15½-ounce / 439-g) can pinto beans
1 (15¼-ounce / 432-g) can

corn
¼ cup brown sugar
1 cup ketchup
1 tablespoon vinegar
2 teaspoons prepared mustard
1 medium onion, chopped

1. Combine all ingredients in crock pot . 2. Cover. Cook on high 3 to 4 hours.

Cheesy Pizza Rice

Prep time: 5 minutes | Cook time: 6 to 10 hours | Serves 6

2 cups rice, uncooked
3 cups chunky pizza sauce
2½ cups water
1 (7-ounce / 170-g) can

mushrooms, undrained
4 ounces (113 g) pepperoni, sliced
1 cup shredded cheese

1. Combine rice, sauce, water, mushrooms, and pepperoni. Stir. 2. Cover. Cook on low 10 hours, or on high 6 hours.

Sprinkle with cheese before serving.

Red Beans and Rice

Prep time: 20 minutes | Cook time: 7 hours | Serves 10

7 cups chicken or seafood stock
1 pound (454 g) dried red beans
½ teaspoon olive oil
¾ pound (340 g) smoked turkey sausage, cut into thin slices
3 celery stalks, chopped
1 green bell pepper, chopped
1 red bell pepper, chopped
1 sweet onion, chopped
3 garlic cloves, minced

1½ teaspoons paprika
1 teaspoon sea salt
½ teaspoon black pepper
1 teaspoon garlic powder
½ teaspoon onion powder
½ teaspoon cayenne pepper
½ teaspoon dried oregano
½ teaspoon dried thyme
hot sauce (optional)
Green onions, finely chopped, for garnish (optional)
Red onion, finely chopped, for garnish (optional)

1. Pour the stock and red beans into the crock pot. 2. Heat olive oil in a medium skillet over medium-high heat. Add the sausage slices and cook until browned, about 4 minutes. Remove from heat. 3. Add the celery, green bell pepper, red bell pepper, chopped onion, garlic, and browned sausage to the crock pot. Stir to combine. Season with paprika, 1 teaspoon salt, ½ teaspoon black pepper, garlic powder, onion powder, cayenne, oregano, and thyme. Mix well. 4. Cover and cook on high for 7 hours, or until the beans are tender. Adjust seasoning with hot sauce or more salt and pepper, to taste. 5. Serve the red bean mixture over hot cooked rice and garnish with green onions or red onions, if desired.

Cajun Sausage and Beans

Prep time: 10 minutes | Cook time: 8 hours | Serves 4 to 6

1 pound (454 g) smoked sausage, sliced into ¼-inch pieces
1 (16-ounce / 454-g) can red beans
1 (16-ounce / 454-g) can crushed tomatoes with

green chilies
1 cup chopped celery
Half an onion, chopped
2 tablespoons Italian seasoning
Tabasco sauce to taste

1. Place all ingredients into the crock pot and stir to combine. 2. Cover and cook on low for 8 hours. 3. Once cooked, serve and enjoy.

Italian Peas and Rice

Prep time: 15 minutes | Cook time: 2½ to 3½ hours | Serves 6

1½ cups converted long-grain white rice, uncooked
¾ cup chopped onions
2 garlic cloves, minced
2 (14½-ounce / 411-g) cans reduced-sodium chicken broth
⅓ cup water

¾ teaspoon Italian seasoning
½ teaspoon dried basil leaves
½ cup frozen baby peas, thawed
¼ cup grated Parmesan cheese

1. Combine rice, onions, and garlic in crock pot . 2. In saucepan, mix together chicken broth and water. Bring to boil. Add Italian seasoning and basil leaves. Stir into rice mixture. 3. Cover. Cook on low 2 to 3 hours, or until liquid is absorbed. 4. Stir in peas. Cover. Cook 30 minutes. Stir in cheese.

Spinach and Farro Medley

Prep time: 15 minutes | Cook time: 7 hours | Serves 2

Nonstick cooking spray
1 leek, white part only, chopped
1 cup sliced cremini mushrooms
2 garlic cloves, minced
1½ cups farro, rinsed
3 cups vegetable broth

½ teaspoon dried marjoram leaves
½ teaspoon salt
⅛ teaspoon freshly ground black pepper
2 cups baby spinach leaves
⅓ cup grated Parmesan or Romano cheese

1. Spray the crock pot with the nonstick cooking spray. 2. In the crock pot , combine all the ingredients except the spinach and cheese, and stir. 3. Cover and cook on low for 6½ hours, or until the farro is almost tender. 4. Stir in the spinach, cover, and cook on low for about 30 minutes more, until the spinach is wilted and the farro is tender. 5. Stir in the cheese and serve.

Four Zesty Beans

Prep time: 5 minutes | Cook time: 2 to 2½ hours | Serves 10

2 (15½-ounce / 439-g) cans Great Northern beans, rinsed and drained
2 (15-ounce / 425-g) cans black beans, rinsed and drained
1 (15-ounce / 425-g) can butter beans, rinsed and drained

1 (15-ounce / 425-g) can baked beans, undrained
2 cups salsa
½ cup brown sugar

1. In the crock pot, combine Great Northern beans, black beans, butter beans, and baked beans. 2. Stir in the salsa and brown sugar, mixing well. 3. Cover and cook on low for 2 to 2½ hours, until heated through.

BBQ Lentils and Veggie Dogs

Prep time: 5 minutes | Cook time: 6 to 8 hours | Serves 8

2 cups barbecue sauce
3½ cups water

1 pound (454 g) dry lentils
1 package vegetarian hot dogs, sliced

1. Combine all ingredients in crock pot . 2. Cover. Cook on low 6 to 8 hours.

Chili Boston Baked Beans

Prep time: 15 minutes | Cook time: 6 to 8 hours | Serves 20

1 cup raisins

2 small onions, diced

2 tart apples, diced

1 cup chili sauce

1 cup chopped ham or crumbled bacon

2 (15-ounce / 425-g) cans baked beans

3 teaspoons dry mustard

½ cup sweet pickle relish

1. Combine all the ingredients in the crock pot and mix well. 2. Cover and cook on low for 6 to 8 hours, allowing the flavors to meld and everything to cook through.

Hometown Spanish Rice

Prep time: 20 minutes | Cook time: 2 to 4 hours | Serves 6 to 8

1 large onion, chopped

1 bell pepper, chopped

1 pound (454 g) bacon, cooked, and broken into bite-size pieces

2 cups long-grain rice, cooked

1 (28-ounce / 794-g) can stewed tomatoes with juice

Grated Parmesan cheese (optional)

Nonstick cooking spray

1. In a small nonstick frying pan, sauté the onion and pepper over medium heat until they become tender. 2. Lightly coat the interior of the crock pot with nonstick cooking spray. 3. Add all ingredients into the crock pot, stirring to combine. 4. Cover and cook on low for 4 hours, or on high for 2 hours, until the dish is heated through. 5. If desired, sprinkle with Parmesan cheese just before serving for an extra touch of flavor.

Chapter 7

Snacks and Appetizers

Chipotle Cheese Dip

Prep time: 20 minutes | Cook time: 2 to 3 hours | Serves 8

1 (8-ounce / 227-g) package cream cheese, cut into cubes

2 tablespoons unsalted butter

1 medium sweet onion, such as Vidalia, finely chopped

4 chipotle chiles in adobo, minced

1 medium red bell pepper, seeded and finely chopped

1 medium yellow bell pepper, seeded and finely chopped

2 teaspoons ground cumin

2 cups finely shredded sharp Cheddar cheese

2 cups finely shredded Monterey Jack cheese

Fresh vegetables for serving

Tortilla chips for serving

1. Coat the insert of a 1½- to 3-quart crock pot with nonstick cooking spray. Turn the machine on low and add the cream cheese. Cover and let stand while preparing the other ingredients. 2. Melt the butter in a large sauté pan over medium-high heat. Add the onion, chipotles, bell peppers, and cumin and sauté until the bell peppers become softened, 4 to 5 minutes. Transfer the contents of the sauté pan into the slow-cooker insert and stir to blend with the cream cheese. 3. Fold in the Cheddar and Jack cheeses. Cover and cook on low for 2 to 3 hours. 4. Serve from the cooker set on warm with fresh vegetables and sturdy tortilla chips.

Orange Chipotle Wings

Prep time: 15 minutes | Cook time: 3 hours | Serves 8

3 pounds (1.4 kg) chicken wing drumettes

1 medium red onion, finely chopped

6 chipotle chiles in adobo, finely chopped

1 teaspoon ground cumin

2 cloves garlic, minced

1½ cups orange juice

½ cup honey

½ cup ketchup

½ cup finely chopped fresh cilantro

1. Lightly grease the insert of a 5- to 7-quart crock pot with nonstick cooking spray. 2. Place the wings on a rack in a baking sheet and broil them on one side until crispy. 3. Flip the wings over and broil for another 5 minutes until both sides are golden and crispy. 4. Remove the wings from the oven. If you prefer, you can refrigerate them for up to 2 days at this point. Otherwise, transfer the wings to the prepared slow-cooker insert. 5. In a mixing bowl, combine the remaining ingredients and pour the sauce over the wings. Toss the wings to coat them evenly. 6. Cover the crock pot and cook the wings on high for 3 hours, turning them twice during the cooking time for even cooking. 7. Serve the wings directly from the slow cooker, keeping it on the warm setting.

Kielbasa in Spicy Barbecue Sauce

Prep time: 20 minutes | Cook time: 4 to 5 hours | Serves 8

2 cups ketchup

½ cup firmly packed light brown sugar

1 tablespoon Worcestershire sauce

1 teaspoon Creole mustard

1 teaspoon hot sauce

1 medium onion, finely chopped

½ cup bourbon

2 pounds (907 g) kielbasa or other smoked sausages, cut into ½-inch rounds

1. Place all the ingredients in the insert of a 3- to 5-quart crock pot. 2. Cover and cook on low for 4 to 5 hours, until the sausage is fully heated through. 3. Serve the kielbasa directly from the cooker, set to warm, with 6-inch skewers for easy serving.

Roasted Tomato and Mozzarella Bruschetta

Prep time: 15 minutes | Cook time: 5 hours | Serves 8

¼ cup extra-virgin olive oil

1 large red onion, coarsely chopped

2 teaspoons dried basil

1 teaspoon fresh rosemary leaves, finely chopped

4 cloves garlic, minced

3 (28- to 32-ounce / 794-

to 907-g) cans whole plum tomatoes, drained

2 teaspoons salt

⅛ teaspoon red pepper flakes

8 ounces (227 g) fresh Mozzarella, cut into ½-inch dice

1. Start by lightly toasting the baguette slices for serving. 2. In the insert of a 5- to 7-quart crock pot, combine all the ingredients except for the Mozzarella and baguette slices. Cover and cook on high for 2 hours. Then, uncover and reduce the heat to low, stirring occasionally, and cook for an additional 3 hours, until most of the tomato liquid has evaporated. 3. Transfer the tomato mixture to a food processor and pulse five times to chop the tomatoes and garlic. Place the mixture into a serving bowl to cool, then stir in the Mozzarella. 4. Serve the dip with the toasted baguette slices.

Curried Almond Snack

Prep time: 5 minutes | Cook time: 3 to 4½ hours | Makes 4 cups nuts

2 tablespoons butter, melted	½ teaspoon seasoned salt
1 tablespoon curry powder	1 pound (454 g) blanched almonds

1. Combine butter with curry powder and seasoned salt. 2. Pour over almonds in crock pot . Mix to coat well. 3. Cover. Cook on low 2 to 3 hours. Turn to high. Uncover cooker and cook 1 to 1½ hours. 4. Serve hot or cold.

Buffalo Chicken Dip

Prep time: 20 minutes | Cook time: 2 hours | Makes 6 cups

2 (8-ounce / 227-g) packages cream cheese, softened	2 cups shredded cooked chicken
½ cup ranch salad dressing	½ cup Buffalo wing sauce
½ cup sour cream	2 cups shredded cheddar cheese, divided
5 tablespoons crumbled blue cheese	1 green onion, sliced
	Tortilla chips

1. In a small bowl, combine the cream cheese, dressing, sour cream and blue cheese. Transfer to a 3-quart crock pot . Layer with chicken, wing sauce and 1 cup cheese. Cover and cook on low for 2 to 3 hours or until heated through. 2. Sprinkle with remaining cheese and onion. Serve with tortilla chips.

Mornay Dip for Crab Claws and Shrimp

Prep time: 10 minutes | Cook time: 2 to 3 hours | Serves 8

2 tablespoons unsalted butter	flour
2 medium shallots, finely chopped	2 cups lobster stock
2 teaspoons Old Bay seasoning	¼ cup cream sherry
2 tablespoons all-purpose	1 cup heavy cream
	¼ cup finely chopped fresh Italian parsley

1. In a small saucepan, melt the butter over medium-high heat. Add the shallots and seasonings, cooking for about 2 minutes until the shallots soften. Stir in the flour and cook for another 3 minutes, whisking constantly. Gradually add the stock and sherry, bringing the mixture to a boil. 2. Once boiling, stir in the cream and parsley, mixing until combined. Pour the mixture into the insert of a 1½- to 3-quart crock pot. Cover and cook on low for 2 to 3 hours. 3. Serve the dish directly from the slow cooker, set on warm.

Crispy Snack Mix

Prep time: 10 minutes | Cook time: 2½ hours | Makes about 2½ quarts

4½ cups crispy chow mein noodles	toasted
4 cups Rice Chex	½ cup butter, melted
1 (9¾-ounce / 276-g) can salted cashews	2 tablespoons reduced-sodium soy sauce
1 cup flaked coconut,	2¼ teaspoons curry powder
	¾ teaspoon ground ginger

1. In the insert of a 5-quart crock pot, combine the noodles, cereal, cashews, and coconut. In a separate bowl, whisk together the butter, soy sauce, curry powder, and ginger. Drizzle this mixture over the cereal blend and toss to coat evenly. 2. Cover the crock pot and cook on low for 2½ hours, stirring every 30 minutes to ensure even cooking. Serve the dish warm or at room temperature.

Hot Broccoli Dip

Prep time: 20 minutes | Cook time: 1 hour | Serves 24

2 cups fresh or frozen broccoli, chopped	containers ranch dip
4 tablespoons chopped red bell pepper	½ cup grated Parmesan cheese
2 (8-ounce / 227-g)	2 cups shredded Cheddar cheese

1. Combine all ingredients in the crock pot. 2. Cover and cook on low for 1 hour. 3. Serve immediately.

Cheddar and Chili Casserole

Prep time: 15 minutes | Cook time: 6 to 8 hours | Serves 8

1¼ cups milk	chopped green chilies
4 eggs, beaten	2 cups shredded Cheddar cheese
3 tablespoons flour	
1 (12-ounce / 340-g) can	

1. Combine all ingredients in crock pot until well blended. 2. Cover and cook on low for 6 to 8 hours. 3. Serve.

Spicy Shrimp Bloody Mary Dip

Prep time: 15 minutes | Cook time: 3 to 4 hours | Serves 8

2 (8-ounce / 227-g) packages cream cheese at room temperature, cut into cubes
1½ cups Clamato juice
2 cups spicy tomato juice or bloody Mary mix
2 tablespoons prepared horseradish
⅓ cup Worcestershire sauce
1 teaspoon Tabasco sauce
2 teaspoons celery salt
¼ teaspoon freshly ground black pepper
2 tablespoons fresh lemon juice
1 cup pepper vodka
4 green onions, finely chopped, using the white and tender green parts
4 stalks celery, finely chopped

1. Coat the insert of a 3- to 5-quart crock pot with nonstick cooking spray. Put the cream cheese in the insert, cover, and cook on low for 20 minutes, until the cream cheese begins to melt. Add the remaining ingredients and stir to combine. 2. Cover and cook on low for 3 to 4 hours, stirring a few times during the cooking time. 3. Serve from the cooker set on warm.

Veggie and Cheese Party Dip

Prep time: 1 hour | Cook time: 1 hour | Makes 5 cups

¾ cup finely chopped fresh broccoli
½ cup finely chopped cauliflower
½ cup finely chopped fresh carrot
½ cup finely chopped red onion
½ cup finely chopped celery
2 garlic cloves, minced
4 tablespoons olive oil, divided
1 (14-ounce / 397-g) can water-packed artichoke hearts, rinsed, drained and chopped
1 (6½-ounce / 184-g) package spreadable garlic
and herb cream cheese
1 (1.4-ounce / 40-g) package vegetable recipe mix (Knorr)
1 teaspoon garlic powder
½ teaspoon white pepper
⅛ to ¼ teaspoon cayenne pepper
¼ cup vegetable broth
¼ cup half-and-half cream
3 cups shredded Italian cheese blend
½ cup minced fresh basil
1 (9-ounce / 255-g) package fresh spinach, finely chopped
Assorted crackers or baked pita chips

1. In a large skillet, saute the broccoli, cauliflower, carrot, onion, celery and garlic in 2 tablespoons oil until tender.

Stir in the artichokes, cream cheese, vegetable recipe mix, garlic powder, white pepper and cayenne; set aside. 2. In a 3-quart crock pot , combine broth, cream and remaining oil. Stir in broccoli mixture, Italian cheese blend and basil. Fold in spinach. Cover and cook on low for 1 to 2 hours or until cheese is melted and spinach is tender. Serve with crackers.

Spicy Sausage Refried Bean Dip

Prep time: 20 minutes | Cook time: 2 to 3 hours | Serves 8

8 ounces (227 g) spicy sausages, such as chorizo, andouille, or Italian, removed from its casing
1 medium onion, chopped
2 Anaheim chiles, seeded and chopped
1 medium red or yellow bell pepper, seeded and chopped
2 (14- to 15-ounce / 397- to
425-g) cans refried beans (nonfat are fine here)
2 cups finely shredded mild Cheddar cheese, or 1 cup each finely shredded Monterey Jack and sharp Cheddar cheese
2 tablespoons finely chopped fresh cilantro
Tortilla chips for serving

1. Spray the insert of a 1½ - to 3-quart crock pot with nonstick cooking spray. Cook the sausage in a medium skillet over high heat until it is no longer pink, breaking up any large pieces with the side of a spoon. Drain the sausage and put it in a mixing bowl to cool. Add the onion, chiles, and bell pepper to the same skillet and sauté until the bell pepper is softened, about 5 minutes. Add to the bowl with the sausage and allow to cool slightly. Add the refried beans to the bowl and stir to blend. 2. Spoon half the bean mixture into the slow-cooker insert and sprinkle with half the cheese. Top with the remaining beans and cheese and sprinkle with the cilantro. Cover and cook on low for 2 to 3 hours. 3. Serve from the cooker set at warm and accompany with sturdy tortilla chips.

Savory Meatball Appetizer

Prep time: 5 minutes | Cook time: 2 hours | Serves 24

1 cup tomato sauce
1 teaspoon Worcestershire sauce
½ teaspoon prepared
mustard
2 tablespoons brown sugar
1 pound (454 g) prepared meatballs or mini-wieners

1. Mix first four ingredients in crock pot . 2. Add meatballs or mini-wieners. 3. Cover and cook on high for 2 hours. Turn to low and serve as an appetizer from the crock pot .

Sweet and Spicy Peanuts

Prep time: 10 minutes | Cook time: 1½ hours | Makes 4 cups

3 cups salted peanuts
½ cup sugar
⅓ cup packed brown sugar
2 tablespoons hot water
2 tablespoons butter,

melted
1 tablespoon Sriracha Asian hot chili sauce or hot pepper sauce
1 teaspoon chili powder

1. Grease a 1½-quart crock pot and add the peanuts. 2. In a separate bowl, mix together the sugars, water, butter, hot sauce, and chili powder. Pour this mixture over the peanuts. Cover and cook on high for 1½ hours, stirring once halfway through. 3. Once cooked, spread the peanuts onto waxed paper to cool. Store in an airtight container.

Swiss Cheese Fondue

Prep time: 10 minutes | Cook time: 2 hours | Makes 3 cups

4 cups shredded Swiss cheese
1 (10¾-ounce / 305-g) can condensed cheddar cheese soup, undiluted
2 tablespoons sherry or chicken broth
1 tablespoon Dijon

mustard
2 garlic cloves, minced
2 teaspoons hot pepper sauce
Cubed French bread baguette
Sliced apples
Seedless red grapes

1. In a 1½-quart crock pot , mix the first six ingredients. Cook, covered, on low 2 to 2½ hours or until the cheese is melted, stirring every 30 minutes. Serve warm with bread cubes and fruit.

Maytag Blue and Walnut Dip with Apple Dippers

Prep time: 10 minutes | Cook time: 2 to 3 hours | Serves 8

2 (8-ounce / 227-g) packages cream cheese at room temperature
½ cup mayonnaise
2 tablespoons Ruby Port
6 drops Tabasco sauce
1 cup chopped walnuts

2 cups crumbled Maytag blue cheese
4 to 6 Granny Smith Apples, cored and cut into 8 wedges each, for serving
Crackers for serving

1. Spray the insert of a 1½- to 3-quart crock pot with nonstick

cooking spray. In a mixing bowl, combine the cream cheese, mayonnaise, port, Tabasco, walnuts, and blue cheese. Stir until well-blended. 2. Transfer the mixture into the crock pot and cover. Cook on low for 2 to 3 hours, until the dip is heated through and bubbly. 3. Serve warm directly from the cooker, alongside apple wedges and crackers.

Artichoke Spinach Bacon Dip

Prep time: 15 minutes | Cook time: 2 to 3 hours | Serves 8

6 strips bacon, cut into ½-inch pieces
1 medium onion, finely chopped
1 (16-ounce / 454-g) package frozen chopped spinach, defrosted and drained thoroughly
1 (16-ounce / 454-g) package frozen artichoke hearts, defrosted, drained,

and coarsely chopped, or
2 (14- to 15-ounce / 397- to 425-g) cans artichoke hearts, drained and coarsely chopped
¼ teaspoon freshly ground black pepper
1½ cups mayonnaise
2 cups shredded sharp white Cheddar cheese

1. Cook the bacon in a large skillet until crisp and remove it to paper towels to drain. Remove all but 2 tablespoons of the bacon drippings from the pan and heat over medium-high heat. 2. Add the onion and sauté until it begins to soften, about 2 minutes. Add the spinach and artichoke hearts and sauté until the water in the pan has evaporated. Season the mixture with the pepper and turn it out into the insert of a 1½- to 3-quart crock pot . Add the mayonnaise and cheese to the cooker and stir until blended. Cover and cook on low for 2 to 3 hours. 3. Garnish the dip with the bacon bits and serve from the cooker set on warm.

Hot Dill and Swiss Dip

Prep time: 10 minutes | Cook time: 2 to 3 hours | Serves 8

2 medium sweet onions, such as Vidalia, finely chopped
2 tablespoons finely chopped fresh dill

1½ cups mayonnaise
2 cups finely shredded Havarti with dill
2 cups finely shredded Swiss cheese

1. Lightly spray the insert of a 1½- to 3-quart crock pot with nonstick cooking spray. In a bowl, combine all the ingredients and transfer the mixture to the crock pot. 2. Cover and cook on low for 2 to 3 hours, or until the mixture is bubbling. 3. Serve directly from the cooker, keeping it set on warm.

Spicy Crocked Nuts

Prep time: 15 minutes | Cook time: 2 to 2½ hours | Serves 8

4 tablespoons (½ stick) unsalted butter, melted
2 teaspoons Lawry's seasoned salt
1 teaspoon garlic salt

⅛ teaspoon cayenne pepper
4 tablespoons sugar
4 cups pecan halves, walnut halves, or whole almonds

1. In the insert of a 5- to 7-quart crock pot, combine the butter, seasoned salt, garlic salt, cayenne pepper, and 2 tablespoons of sugar. Cover and cook on high for 20 minutes. 2. Add the nuts to the crock pot and stir well to coat them in the butter mixture. Cook uncovered for 2 to 2½ hours, stirring occasionally. 3. Once the nuts are cooked, sprinkle the remaining 2 tablespoons of sugar over them, toss to coat, and transfer the nuts to a baking sheet. Allow them to cool completely before serving.

Wine-Glazed Sausages

Prep time: 15 minutes | Cook time: 1 hour | Serves 6

1 cup dry red wine
2 tablespoons currant jelly

6 to 8 mild Italian sausages or Polish sausages

1. Place wine and jelly in crock pot . Heat until jelly is dissolved and sauce begins to simmer. Add sausages. 2. Cover and cook on high 45 minutes to 1 hour, or until sausages are cooked through and lightly glazed. 3. Transfer sausages to a cutting board and slice. Serve.

Reuben Spread

Prep time: 10 minutes | Cook time: 4 hours | Serves 3

2 (8-ounce / 227-g) packages cream cheese, cubed
4 cups shredded Swiss cheese
1 (14-ounce / 397-g) can sauerkraut, rinsed and well drained

4 (2-ounce / 57-g) packages thinly sliced deli corned beef, chopped
½ cup Thousand Island salad dressing
Snack rye bread or rye crackers

1. In a 1½-quart crock pot, combine the first five ingredients and stir to mix. Cover and cook on low for 4 to 4½ hours, or until heated through. 2. Stir the mixture to blend, and serve as a spread on bread.

Easy Barbecue Smokies

Prep time: 5 minutes | Cook time: 2 hours | Serves 12 to 16

1 (18-ounce / 510-g) bottle barbecue sauce
8 ounces (227 g) salsa

2 (16-ounce / 454-g) packages little smokies

1. Combine the barbecue sauce and salsa in the crock pot. 2. Add the little smokies and stir to coat. 3. Cook on high for 2 hours. 4. Stir, then reduce to low to keep warm while serving.

Spinach Leek Dip

Prep time: 10 minutes | Cook time: 1 hour | Serves 12

2 cups fat-free sour cream
¼ cup fat-free miracle whip salad dressing
1 (10-ounce / 283-g) package frozen chopped spinach, squeezed dry and

chopped
1 (1.8-ounce / 51-g) envelope dry leek soup mix
¼ cup red bell pepper, minced

1. Combine all ingredients in crock pot . Mix well. 2. Cover. Cook on high 1 hour. 3. Serve.

Crocked Candy

Prep time: 10 minutes | Cook time: 2 hours | Makes 80 to 100 pieces

1½ pounds (680 g) almond bark, broken
1 (4-ounce / 113-g) Baker's Brand German sweet chocolate bar, broken
8 ounces (227 g) chocolate

chips
8 ounces (227 g) peanut butter chips
2 pounds (907 g) lightly salted or unsalted peanuts

1. Begin by spraying the inside of the crock pot with nonstick cooking spray. 2. Layer the ingredients in the crock pot in the order listed above. 3. Cover and cook on low for 2 hours. Avoid stirring or lifting the lid during the cooking time. 4. After 2 hours, mix everything together thoroughly. 5. Drop the mixture by teaspoonfuls onto waxed paper. Refrigerate for about 45 minutes before serving or storing.

Pizza Cheese Fondue

Prep time: 15 minutes | Cook time: 1 hour | Serves 4 to 6

1 (1-pound / 454-g) block of cheese, your choice of good melting cheese, cut in ½-inch cubes
2 cups shredded Mozzarella cheese
1 (19-ounce / 539-g) can Italian-style stewed tomatoes with juice
Loaf of Italian bread, slices toasted and then cut into 1-inch cubes

1. Place cheese cubes, shredded Mozzarella cheese, and tomatoes in a lightly greased crock pot . 2. Cover and cook on high 45 to 60 minutes, or until cheese is melted. 3. Stir occasionally and scrape down sides of crock pot with rubber spatula to prevent scorching. 4. Reduce heat to low and serve. (Fondue will keep a smooth consistency for up to 4 hours.) 5. Serve with toasted bread cubes for dipping.

Sweet 'n Sour Meatballs

Prep time: 10 minutes | Cook time: 2 to 4 hours | Serves 15 to 20

1 (12-ounce / 340-g) jar grape jelly
1 (12-ounce / 340-g) jar chili sauce
2 (1-pound / 454-g) bags prepared frozen meatballs, thawed

1. In the crock pot, mix the jelly and sauce together, stirring until well combined. 2. Add the meatballs and stir to coat them evenly. 3. Cover and cook on low for 4 hours or on high for 2 hours. Keep the crock pot on low while serving.

Cranberry Chutney Baked Brie

Prep time: 10 minutes | Cook time: 4 hours | Serves 8 to 10

1 cup fresh or dried cranberries
½ cup brown sugar
⅓ cup cider vinegar
2 tablespoons water or orange juice
2 teaspoons minced crystallized ginger
¼ teaspoon cinnamon
⅛ teaspoon ground cloves
Oil
1 (8-ounce / 227-g) round of Brie cheese
1 tablespoon sliced almonds, toasted
Crackers

1. Mix together cranberries, brown sugar, vinegar, water or juice, ginger, cinnamon, and cloves in crock pot . 2. Cover. Cook on low 4 hours. Stir once near the end to see if it is thickening. If not, remove lid, turn heat to high and cook 30 minutes without lid. 3. Put cranberry chutney in covered container and chill for up to 2 weeks. When ready to serve, bring to room temperature. 4. Brush ovenproof plate with oil, place unpeeled Brie on plate, and bake uncovered at 350ºF (180ºC) for 9 minutes, until cheese is soft and partially melted. Remove from oven. 5. Top with at least half the chutney and garnish with almonds. Serve with crackers.

Creamy Artichoke Dip

Prep time: 20 minutes | Cook time: 1 hour | Makes 5 cups

2 (14-ounce / 397-g) cans water-packed artichoke hearts, rinsed, drained and coarsely chopped
2 cups shredded part-skim mozzarella cheese
1 (8-ounce / 227-g) package cream cheese, cubed
1 cup shredded Parmesan cheese
½ cup mayonnaise
½ cup shredded Swiss cheese
2 tablespoons lemon juice
2 tablespoons plain yogurt
1 tablespoon seasoned salt
1 tablespoon chopped seeded jalapeno pepper
1 teaspoon garlic powder
Tortilla chips

1. In a 3-quart crock pot, combine the first 11 ingredients and stir to mix them well. 2. Cover and cook on low for 1 hour, or until heated through. 3. Serve with tortilla chips for dipping.

Chicken Liver Paté

Prep time: 15 minutes | Cook time: 4 to 5 hours | Makes 1½ cups paté

1 pound (454 g) chicken livers
½ cup dry wine
1 teaspoon instant chicken bouillon
1 teaspoon minced parsley
1 tablespoon instant
minced onion
¼ teaspoon ground ginger
½ teaspoon seasoned salt
1 tablespoon soy sauce
¼ teaspoon dry mustard
¼ cup soft butter
1 tablespoon brandy

1. In crock pot , combine all ingredients except butter and brandy. 2. Cover. Cook on low 4 to 5 hours. Let stand in liquid until cool. 3. Drain. Place in blender or food grinder. Add butter and brandy. Process until smooth. 4. Serve.

Chapter 8

Vegetables and Sides

Pomegranate Roasted Beets with Goat Cheese

Prep time: 15 minutes | Cook time: 5 hours | Serves 6 to 8

6 to 8 medium beets, scrubbed, stem ends trimmed

1 cup canola or vegetable oil

½ cup pomegranate juice

¼ cup rice vinegar

2 shallots, finely chopped

2 teaspoons sugar

1 teaspoon salt

½ teaspoon freshly ground black pepper

¼ cup thinly sliced fresh basil, for garnish

8 ounces (227 g) goat cheese, crumbled, for garnish

1. Wrap each beet individually in aluminum foil and arrange in the insert of a 5- to 7-quart crock pot . Cover and cook on high for 5 hours, until the tip of a knife inserted into the thickest part of the beet goes in without any resistance. 2. Remove the beets from the slow-cooker insert and allow them to cool. Unwrap the beets and slip the skins off with a sharp paring knife. 3. Cut the beets into wedges and transfer to a bowl. Whisk together the oil, pomegranate juice, vinegar, shallots, sugar, salt, and pepper in a mixing bowl. Pour the mixture over the beets and toss to coat. 4. Marinate the beets for at least 2 hours or up to 3 days. 5. Drain the beets and arrange on a serving platter and sprinkle with the basil and goat cheese.

Crocked Ratatouille

Prep time: 20 minutes | Cook time: 4 to 7 hours | Serves 6

1 tablespoon olive oil

1 large onion, chopped

6 large garlic cloves, minced

1 green bell pepper, cut into strips

1 red bell pepper, cut into strips

1 medium eggplant, cubed

2 cups thickly sliced mushrooms

4 tomatoes, cubed

1 cup low-sodium tomato purée

¼ cup dry red wine or wine vinegar

1 tablespoon lemon juice

2 teaspoons dried thyme

1 teaspoon dried oregano

1 teaspoon ground cumin

½ to 1 teaspoon salt

¼ to ½ teaspoon black pepper

4 tablespoons minced fresh basil

¼ cup chopped fresh parsley

1. Preheat the crock pot on high for 2 minutes. 2. Add the oil to the crock pot, then stir in all the remaining ingredients, except for the parsley and fresh basil. 3. Cover and cook on high for 2 hours, then reduce to low and cook for 4 to 5 hours. 4. Stir in the fresh basil, sprinkle with parsley, and serve.

Golden Carrots

Prep time: 5 minutes | Cook time: 3 to 4 hours | Serves 6

1 (2-pound / 907-g) package baby carrots

½ cup golden raisins

1 stick butter, melted or softened

⅓ cup honey

2 tablespoons lemon juice

½ teaspoon ground ginger (optional)

1. Add all ingredients to the crock pot and stir to combine. 2. Cover and cook on low for 3 to 4 hours, or until the carrots are tender-crisp.

Lentil and Rice Stew

Prep time: 10 minutes | Cook time: 10 hours | Serves 20 to 24

10 cups water

4 cups dried lentils, rinsed

2 cups brown rice,

uncooked

¼ cup olive oil

2 teaspoons salt

1. Combine ingredients in large crock pot . 2. Cover. Cook on high 8 hours, then on low 2 hours. Add 2 more cups water, if needed, to allow rice to cook and to prevent dish from drying out. 3. Serve.

Stuffed Mushrooms

Prep time: 20 minutes | Cook time: 2 to 4 hours | Serves 4 to 6

8 to 10 large mushrooms

¼ teaspoon minced garlic

1 tablespoon oil

Dash of salt

Dash of pepper

Dash of cayenne pepper (optional)

¼ cup shredded Monterey Jack cheese

1. Remove the stems from the mushrooms and dice them. 2. Heat oil in a skillet over medium heat and sauté the diced mushroom stems with garlic until softened. Remove from heat. 3. Stir in the seasonings and cheese, then stuff the mixture into the mushroom caps. Arrange the stuffed mushrooms in the crock pot. 4. Cover and cook on low for 2 to 4 hours, until heated through and the mushrooms are tender.

Easy Slow-Cooked Potatoes

Prep time: 10 minutes | Cook time: 4 to 10 hours | Serves 12

12 potatoes
Butter, softened

Nonstick cooking spray

1. Spray crock pot with nonstick cooking spray. 2. Rub butter over unpeeled whole potatoes. Place in crock pot . 3. Cover and cook on high 4 to 5 hours, or on low 8 to 10 hours, or until potatoes are tender when jagged.

Cheesy Squash and Ham Casserole

Prep time: 30 minutes | Cook time: 1½ to 2 hours | Serves 6 to 8

6 medium yellow squash, cut into ½-inch pieces
1 teaspoon salt
4 tablespoons unsalted butter, plus 2 tablespoons, melted
1 medium onion, finely chopped
1 teaspoon dried thyme
¼ cup all-purpose flour
½ cup chicken broth
2 cups heavy cream

1 teaspoon Tabasco sauce
2½ cups finely shredded sharp white or mild Cheddar cheese
1 cup finely chopped ham
10 buttery crackers, crushed (about ½ cup)
¼ cup finely chopped fresh Italian parsley
¼ cup freshly grated Parmesan cheese

1. Coat the insert of a 5- to 7-quart crock pot with nonstick cooking spray or line it with a slow-cooker liner according to the manufacturer's directions. 2. Place the squash in a colander and sprinkle with the salt. Set the squash aside for 30 minutes to drain excess moisture. 3. Melt the 4 tablespoons butter in a medium saucepan over medium-high heat. Add the onion and thyme and sauté until the onion is softened, about 4 minutes. Sprinkle the flour into the saucepan and cook, stirring, for 3 minutes. Stir in the chicken broth, cream, and Tabasco and bring the sauce to a boil, stirring constantly. The sauce should be quite thick. Pour the sauce into the slow-cooker insert and fold in the Cheddar cheese and ham. Press out any excess moisture from the squash with paper towels and add the squash to the slow-cooker insert. Stir to distribute the ingredients. 4. Cover and cook on high for 1½ to 2 hours, until the casserole is heated through and the squash is tender. While the casserole is cooking, stir together the melted butter, crushed crackers, parsley, and Parmesan. 5. Sprinkle the top of the casserole with the buttered cracker crumbs and serve from the cooker set on warm.

Sweet Potatoes and Apples

Prep time: 15 minutes | Cook time: 6 to 8 hours | Serves 8 to 10

3 large sweet potatoes, peeled and cubed
3 large tart and firm apples, peeled and sliced
½ to ¾ teaspoon salt
⅛ to ¼ teaspoon pepper
1 teaspoon sage

1 teaspoon ground cinnamon
4 tablespoons (½ stick) butter, melted
¼ cup maple syrup
Toasted sliced almonds or chopped pecans (optional)

1. Start by layering half of the sweet potatoes in the bottom of the crock pot, then add half of the apple slices on top. 2. In a small bowl, mix together the seasonings and sprinkle half of the mixture over the apples. 3. Combine the butter and maple syrup, then drizzle half of this mixture over the seasoned apples. 4. Repeat the layering process with the remaining sweet potatoes, apples, seasonings, and syrup mixture. 5. Cover and cook on low for 6 to 8 hours, stirring occasionally, until the sweet potatoes are tender. 6. For an added crunch, sprinkle toasted almonds or pecans on top just before serving. 7. Serve warm.

Vegetable Rice Casserole

Prep time: 10 minutes | Cook time: 3 to 4 hours | Serves 8

¼ cup rice, uncooked
1 pound (454 g) zucchini, sliced
1 pound (454 g) yellow summer squash, sliced
1 large onion, sliced
1 tablespoon dried basil, divided
1 medium green bell

pepper, julienned
4 celery ribs with leaves, chopped
2 large tomatoes, sliced
¼ cup packed brown sugar
½ teaspoon salt
¼ teaspoon black pepper
2 tablespoons olive oil
Fat-free cooking spray

1. Coat the crock pot with fat-free cooking spray and spread the rice evenly in the bottom. 2. Layer the zucchini, yellow squash, onion, and half of the basil on top of the rice. 3. Add the green pepper, celery, and tomatoes on top of the previous layers. 4. Mix the brown sugar, salt, and pepper together and sprinkle over the vegetables. Drizzle with olive oil. 5. Cover and cook on high for 3 to 4 hours, or until the vegetables are cooked to your desired tenderness. 6. Once done, sprinkle the remaining basil over the dish before serving.

Vegetable Medley Stir-Fry

Prep time: 20 minutes | Cook time: 8 to 10 hours | Serves 8

1 (16-ounce / 454-g) bag baby carrots
4 ribs celery, chunked
1 medium onion, diced
1 (14½-ounce / 411-g) can low-sodium Italian-style stewed tomatoes
½ teaspoon dried basil
½ teaspoon dried oregano
½ teaspoon salt
1 large red or yellow bell pepper, diced
1 small head cabbage, cut up
1 pound (454 g) raw broccoli, cut up

1. Combine carrots, celery, onion, tomatoes, basil, oregano, and salt in crock pot . 2. Cover. Cook on high 3 to 4 hours, or on low 6 to 8 hours, stirring occasionally. 3. Stir in pepper, cabbage, and broccoli. 4. Cook 1 hour more on high, or 2 hours more on low, stirring occasionally. You may need to add a little water if there is not liquid left on the veggies.

Garlicky Potatoes

Prep time: 10 minutes | Cook time: 5 to 6 hours | Serves 6

6 potatoes, peeled and cubed
6 garlic cloves, minced
¼ cup dried onion, or 1 medium onion, chopped
2 tablespoons olive oil

1. Add all the ingredients to the crock pot and stir to combine. 2. Cover and cook on low for 5 to 6 hours, or until the potatoes are tender but not browned.

Cranberry-Orange Glazed Beets

Prep time: 15 minutes | Cook time: 3½ to 7½ hours | Serves 6

2 pounds (907 g) medium beets, peeled and quartered
½ teaspoon ground nutmeg
1 cup cranberry juice
1 teaspoon orange peel,
finely shredded (optional)
2 tablespoons butter
2 tablespoons sugar
4 teaspoons cornstarch

1. Place beets in crock pot . Sprinkle with nutmeg. 2. Add cranberry juice and orange peel. Dot with butter. 3. Cover. Cook on low 6 to 7 hours, or on high 3 to 3½ hours. 4. In small bowl, combine sugar and cornstarch. 5. Remove ½ cup of cooking liquid and stir into cornstarch. 6. Stir mixture into crock pot . 7. Cover. Cook on high 15 to 30 minutes.

"Baked" Tomatoes

Prep time: 5 minutes | Cook time: ¾ to 1 hour | Serves 4

2 tomatoes, each cut in half
½ tablespoon olive oil
½ teaspoon parsley, chopped, or ¼ teaspoon
dry parsley flakes
¼ teaspoon dried oregano
¼ teaspoon dried basil
Nonfat cooking spray

1. Arrange the tomato halves in the crock pot, spraying the insert with nonfat cooking spray first. 2. Drizzle olive oil over the tomatoes and sprinkle with the remaining ingredients. 3. Cover and cook on high for 45 minutes to 1 hour, until the tomatoes are tender.

Bacon Beans and Potatoes

Prep time: 15 minutes | Cook time: 6 hours | Serves 10

8 bacon strips, chopped
1½ pounds (680 g) fresh green beans, trimmed and cut into 2-inch pieces (about 4 cups)
4 medium potatoes, peeled and cubed (½ inch)
1 small onion, halved and sliced
¼ cup reduced-sodium chicken broth
½ teaspoon salt
¼ teaspoon pepper

1. In a large skillet, cook bacon over medium heat until crisp, stirring occasionally. Remove to paper towels with a slotted spoon; drain, reserving 1 tablespoon drippings. Cover and refrigerate bacon until serving. 2. In a 5-quart crock pot , combine the remaining ingredients; stir in reserved drippings. Cover and cook on low for 6 to 8 hours or until potatoes are tender. Stir in bacon; heat through.

Green Beans with Dill

Prep time: 5 minutes | Cook time: 3 to 4 hours | Serves 8

2 quarts cut green beans, or 4 (14½-ounce / 411-g) cans cut green beans
2 teaspoons beef bouillon
granules
½ teaspoon dill seed
¼ cup water
Fat-free cooking spray

1. Lightly coat the slow cooker with fat-free cooking spray. 2. Add all the ingredients to the cooker and stir to combine. 3. Set the cooker to high and cook for 3 to 4 hours, until fully cooked and heated through.

Bavarian Cabbage

Prep time: 10 minutes | Cook time: 3 to 8 hours | Serves 4 to 8

1 small head red cabbage, sliced

1 medium onion, chopped

3 tart apples, cored and quartered

2 teaspoons salt

1 cup hot water

2 tablespoons sugar

⅓ cup vinegar

3 tablespoons bacon drippings

1. Add all the ingredients to the slow cooker in the order they are listed. 2. Cover and cook on low for 8 hours, or on high for 3 hours. Stir thoroughly before serving to ensure even distribution of flavors.

Sour Cream Zucchini Casserole

Prep time: 10 minutes | Cook time: 1 to 1½ hours | Serves 6

4 cups unpeeled, sliced zucchini

1 cup fat-free sour cream

¼ cup skim milk

1 cup chopped onions

1 teaspoon salt

1 cup shredded low-fat sharp Cheddar cheese

Nonfat cooking spray

1. Parboil zucchini in microwave for 2 to 3 minutes. Turn into crock pot sprayed with nonfat cooking spray. 2. Combine sour cream, milk, onions, and salt. Pour over zucchini and stir gently. 3. Cover. Cook on low 1 to 1½ hours. 4. Sprinkle cheese over vegetables 30 minutes before serving.

Garlic Gorgonzola Green Beans

Prep time: 20 minutes | Cook time: 3 hours | Serves 10

2 pounds (907 g) fresh green beans, trimmed and halved

1 (8-ounce / 227-g) can sliced water chestnuts, drained

4 green onions, chopped

5 bacon strips, cooked and crumbled, divided

⅓ cup white wine or

chicken broth

2 tablespoons minced fresh thyme or 2 teaspoons dried thyme

4 garlic cloves, minced

1½ teaspoons seasoned salt

1 cup sour cream

¾ cup crumbled Gorgonzola cheese

1. Place green beans, water chestnuts, green onions and ¼ cup cooked bacon in a 4-quart crock pot . In a small bowl, mix wine, thyme, garlic and seasoned salt; pour over top. Cook, covered, on low 3 to 4 hours or until green beans are crisp-tender. Drain liquid from beans. 2. Just before serving, stir in sour cream; sprinkle with cheese and remaining bacon.

Fruity Sweet Potatoes

Prep time: 15 minutes | Cook time: 6 to 8 hours | Serves 6

2 pounds (907 g) sweet potatoes or yams

1½ cups applesauce

⅔ cup brown sugar

3 tablespoons butter, melted

1 teaspoon cinnamon

Chopped nuts (optional)

1. Peel the sweet potatoes if desired, then cut them into cubes or slices and place them in the crock pot. 2. In a bowl, combine the applesauce, brown sugar, butter, and cinnamon. Pour this mixture over the sweet potatoes. 3. Cover and cook on low for 6 to 8 hours, or until the potatoes are tender. 4. For a mashed version, use a large spoon to mash the potatoes and sauce together, or simply transfer the potatoes to a serving dish and top with the sauce. 5. Optionally, sprinkle with nuts for added texture before serving.

Stuffed Acorn Squash

Prep time: 15 minutes | Cook time: 2½ hours | Serves 6

3 small carnival or acorn squash

5 tablespoons instant brown rice

3 tablespoons dried cranberries

3 tablespoons diced celery

3 tablespoons minced onion

Pinch of ground or dried sage

1 teaspoon butter, divided

3 tablespoons orange juice

½ cup water

1. Cut off the pointed ends of the squash so they can stand upright in the slow cooker. Remove the tops and discard them, then scoop out the seeds. Arrange the squash in the slow cooker. 2. In a mixing bowl, combine rice, cranberries, chopped celery, diced onion, and sage. Stuff the mixture into the hollowed squash. 3. Place small pats of butter on top of the stuffed squash. 4. Drizzle a tablespoon of orange juice into the center of each squash. 5. Pour water into the bottom of the slow cooker to help create steam. 6. Cover and cook on low for 2½ hours, allowing the flavors to meld together. 7. Once done, remove from the cooker and serve.

Sweet Potato Stuffing

Prep time: 15 minutes | Cook time: 4 hours | Serves 8

½ cup chopped celery
½ cup chopped onions
¼ cup butter
6 cups dry bread cubes
1 large sweet potato, cooked, peeled, and cubed
½ cup chicken broth
¼ cup chopped pecans
½ teaspoon poultry seasoning
½ teaspoon rubbed sage
½ teaspoon salt
¼ teaspoon pepper

1. Sauté the celery and onion in butter in a skillet until tender, then transfer them to a greased crock pot. 2. Add the remaining ingredients to the crock pot and toss everything gently to combine. 3. Cover and cook on low for 4 hours, until the vegetables are fully cooked.

Balsamic Summer Vegetable Medley

Prep time: 15 minutes | Cook time: 6 hours | Serves 6

½ cup extra-virgin olive oil
¼ cup balsamic vinegar
1 tablespoon dried basil
1 teaspoon dried thyme
¼ teaspoon salt
2 cups cauliflower florets
2 zucchini, diced into 1-inch pieces
1 yellow bell pepper, cut into strips
1 cup halved button mushrooms

1. In a large bowl, whisk together the oil, vinegar, basil, thyme, and salt, until blended. 2. Add the cauliflower, zucchini, bell pepper, and mushrooms, and toss to coat. 3. Transfer the vegetables to the insert of a crock pot . 4. Cover and cook on low for 6 hours. 5. Serve.

Crispy Pancetta Brussels Sprouts

Prep time: 10 minutes | Cook time: 1½ hours | Serves 6

½ cup extra-virgin olive oil
3 ounces (85 g) pancetta, finely chopped
3 cloves garlic, sliced
2 pounds (907 g) Brussels sprouts, ends trimmed, cut
into quarters, and leaves separated
1½ teaspoons salt
½ teaspoon freshly ground black pepper

1. Heat the oil in a medium sauté pan over high heat. Add the pancetta and cook until crispy. Remove it to paper towels to drain. Add the garlic to the pan and cook over low heat until it begins to turn golden, being careful not to let it get brown. 2. Pour the oil and garlic into the insert of a 5- to 7-quart crock pot . Stir in the sprouts, salt, and pepper. cover and cook on high for 1 hour, until the leaves are tender. Stir in the pancetta and cook for another 30 minutes. 3. Serve hot or at room temperature.

Italian Eggplant Casserole

Prep time: 20 minutes | Cook time: 4 hours | Serves 6 to 8

2 eggplants
¼ cup eggbeaters
24 ounces (680 g) fat-free cottage cheese
¼ teaspoon salt
Black pepper to taste
1 (14-ounce / 397-g) tomato sauce
2 to 4 tablespoons Italian seasoning, according to your taste preference

1. Peel eggplants and cut in ½-inch-thick slices. Soak in salt-water for about 5 minutes to remove bitterness. Drain well. 2. Spray crock pot with fat-free cooking spray. 3. Mix eggbeaters, cottage cheese, salt, and pepper together in bowl. 4. Mix tomato sauce and Italian seasoning together in another bowl. 5. Spoon a thin layer of tomato sauce into bottom of crock pot . Top with about one-third of the eggplant slices, and then one-third of the egg-cheese mixture, and finally one-third of the remaining tomato sauce mixture. 6. Repeat those layers twice, ending with seasoned tomato sauce. 7. Cover. Cook on high 4 hours. Allow to rest 15 minutes before serving.

Creamy Hash Browns

Prep time: 10 minutes | Cook time: 4 to 5 hours | Serves 14

1 (30-ounce / 850-g) package frozen, diced hash browns
2 cups cubed or shredded cheese of your choice
2 cups sour cream
2 (10¾-ounce / 305-g) cans cream of chicken soup
Half a stick (¼ cup) butter, melted

1. Start by layering the hash browns at the bottom of an ungreased slow cooker. 2. In a separate bowl, mix together the remaining ingredients and pour the mixture evenly over the potatoes. Stir to combine everything well. 3. Cover the slow cooker and cook on low for 4 to 5 hours, or until the potatoes are tender and fully heated.

Sausage and Bacon Stuffing

Prep time: 25 minutes | Cook time: 4 hours | Serves 20

1 pound (454 g) bulk pork sausage
1 pound (454 g) thick-sliced bacon strips, chopped
½ cup butter, cubed
1 large onion, chopped
3 celery ribs, sliced
10½ cups unseasoned stuffing cubes
1 cup sliced fresh mushrooms
1 cup chopped fresh parsley
4 teaspoons dried sage leaves
4 teaspoons dried thyme
6 eggs
2 (10¾-ounce / 305-g) cans condensed cream of chicken soup, undiluted
1¼ cups chicken stock

1. In a large skillet, cook sausage over medium heat for 6 to 8 minutes or until no longer pink, breaking into crumbles. Remove with a slotted spoon; drain on paper towels. Discard drippings. 2. Add bacon to pan; cook over medium heat until crisp. Remove to paper towels to drain. Discard drippings. Wipe out pan. In same pan, heat butter over medium-high heat. Add onion and celery; cook and stir 6 to 8 minutes or until tender. Remove from heat. 3. In a large bowl, combine stuffing cubes, sausage, bacon, onion mixture, mushrooms, parsley, sage and thyme. In a small bowl, whisk eggs, soup and stock; pour over stuffing mixture and toss to coat. 4. Transfer to a greased 6-quart crock pot . Cook, covered, on low 4 to 5 hours or until a thermometer reads 160ºF (71ºC). Remove lid; let stand 15 minutes before serving.

Swiss-Irish Hot Sauce

Prep time: 15 minutes | Cook time: 4 hours | Serves 6 to 8

2 medium onions, diced
5 garlic cloves, minced
¼ cup oil
1 (1-pound / 454-g) can tomatoes, puréed
1 (15-ounce / 425-g) can tomato sauce
1 (12-ounce / 340-g) can tomato paste
2 tablespoons parsley, fresh
or dried
½ teaspoon red pepper
½ teaspoon black pepper
1 teaspoon chili powder
1 teaspoon dried basil
2 teaspoons Worcestershire sauce
2 teaspoons Tabasco sauce
¼ cup red wine

1. In a skillet, sauté the onions and garlic in oil until softened and fragrant. 2. Transfer all the ingredients into the slow cooker and mix to combine. 3. Cover and cook on low for 4 hours, allowing the flavors to meld together. 4. Once done, serve and enjoy.

Crocked Baked Potatoes

Prep time: 10 minutes | Cook time: 3 to 8 hours | Serves 8 to 10

8 russet baking potatoes, scrubbed
½ cup extra-virgin olive oil
1 tablespoon salt
1 teaspoon coarsely ground black pepper

1. Prick each potato several times with the tip of a sharp knife. Combine the oil, salt, and pepper in a bowl and rub the potatoes all over the oil mixture. 2. Arrange the potatoes in the insert of a 5- to 7-quart crock pot . Cover and cook on high for 3 to 4 hours or on low for 7 to 8 hours. 3. Remove the potatoes from the crock pot and serve, or serve from the cooker set on warm.

Potatoes Pizzaiola

Prep time: 30 minutes | Cook time: 5 to 8 hours | Serves 6 to 8

4 tablespoons extra-virgin olive oil
2 cloves garlic, minced
2 teaspoons dried oregano
1 (28- to 32-ounce / 794- to 907-g) can crushed tomatoes
2½ teaspoons salt
1 teaspoon freshly ground black pepper
8 medium red potatoes,
scrubbed and cut into ¼-inch-thick slices
½ medium red onion, cut into thin half rounds (about ¼ cup)
2 cups shredded Mozzarella
1 cup freshly grated Parmigiano-Reggiano cheese

1. Lightly grease the insert of a 5- to 7-quart slow cooker using nonstick spray or a slow-cooker liner as per the instructions. 2. Heat 2 tablespoons of oil in a large saucepan over medium-high heat. Add garlic and oregano, cooking for about 30 seconds until aromatic. 3. Stir in the tomatoes, 1 teaspoon salt, and ½ teaspoon pepper, then let it simmer uncovered for 30 to 45 minutes. Taste and adjust seasoning to your preference. In a separate bowl, toss the potatoes and onion with the remaining salt, pepper, and 2 tablespoons of oil. In another bowl, mix the cheeses together. 4. Begin by spreading ½ to ¾ cup of the tomato sauce on the bottom of the slow cooker insert. Layer half of the potatoes, then sprinkle with half of the cheese, and top with a generous spoonful of sauce. Repeat the layers with the remaining potatoes, cheese, and sauce. 5. Cover the slow cooker and cook on high for 5 hours or low for 8 hours, until the potatoes are tender and cooked through. Serve directly from the slow cooker, keeping it on the warm setting.

Special Spinach Bake

Prep time: 10 minutes | Cook time: 5 hours | Serves 8

3 (10-ounce / 283-g) boxes frozen spinach, thawed and drained
2 cups cottage cheese
1½ cups shredded Cheddar cheese

3 eggs
¼ cup flour
1 teaspoon salt
½ cup butter, or margarine, melted

1. Mix together all ingredients. 2. Pour into crock pot . 3. Cook on high 1 hour. Reduce heat to low and cook 4 more hours.

Cider-Braised Red Cabbage

Prep time: 15 minutes | Cook time: 4 to 5 hours | Serves 6 to 8

2 medium red onions, cut into half rounds
10 cups thinly sliced red cabbage (about 2 large heads)
2 medium Granny Smith apples, peeled, cored, and cut into ½-inch-thick slices

1 cup apple cider or apple juice
2 whole cloves
2 tablespoons light brown sugar
2 tablespoons balsamic vinegar

1. Place all the ingredients into the insert of a 5- to 7-quart slow cooker and toss them together to evenly coat. Cover and cook on low for 4 to 5 hours, or until the cabbage is tender. 2. Remove the cloves, then serve the cabbage directly from the slow cooker, keeping it on the warm setting.

Riesling Braised Cabbage with Caraway

Prep time: 10 minutes | Cook time: 4 to 5 hours | Serves 6 to 8

2 tablespoons olive oil
2 medium sweet onions, finely chopped
2 teaspoons caraway seeds
10 cups thinly sliced green

cabbage (about 2 medium heads)
2 cups Riesling wine
1 teaspoon freshly ground black pepper

1. Heat the oil in a large skillet over medium-high heat. Add the onions and caraway seeds and sauté until the onions are softened, about 3 minutes. Transfer the contents of the skillet to the insert of a 5- to 7-quart crock pot . 2. Add the cabbage, Riesling, and pepper and stir to coat the cabbage

and distribute the ingredients. Cover and cook on low for 4 to 5 hours, until the cabbage is tender. 3. Serve from the cooker set on warm.

Potatoes O'Brien

Prep time: 10 minutes | Cook time: 4 to 5 hours | Serves 6

1 (32-ounce / 907-g) package shredded potatoes
¼ cup chopped onions
¼ cup chopped green peppers
2 tablespoons chopped pimento
1 cup chopped ham
¾ teaspoon salt

¼ teaspoon pepper
3 tablespoons butter
3 tablespoons flour
½ cup milk
1 (10¾-ounce / 305-g) can cream of mushroom soup
1 cup shredded Cheddar cheese, divided

1. Add the potatoes, onions, green peppers, pimentos, and ham to the slow cooker. Season with salt and pepper to taste. 2. In a saucepan, melt the butter, then stir in the flour. Gradually add half of the milk, stirring constantly to eliminate any lumps. Once smooth, add the remaining milk, followed by the mushroom soup and ½ cup of cheese. Stir to combine, then pour the mixture over the potatoes. 3. Cover and cook on low for 4 to 5 hours, until the potatoes are tender. About 30 minutes before serving, sprinkle the remaining cheese on top.

Creamed Vegetables

Prep time: 15 minutes | Cook time: 6 hours | Serves 6

1 tablespoon extra-virgin olive oil
½ head cauliflower, cut into small florets
2 cups green beans, cut into 2-inch pieces
1 cup asparagus spears, cut into 2-inch pieces
½ cup sour cream

½ cup shredded Cheddar cheese
½ cup shredded Swiss cheese
3 tablespoons butter
¼ cup water
1 teaspoon ground nutmeg
Pinch freshly ground black pepper, for seasoning

1. Lightly grease the insert of the slow cooker with olive oil. 2. Add the cauliflower, green beans, asparagus, sour cream, Cheddar cheese, Swiss cheese, butter, water, nutmeg, and pepper to the insert. Stir to combine. 3. Cover and cook on low for 6 hours, allowing the flavors to blend and the vegetables to become tender. 4. Serve warm and enjoy the creamy vegetable dish.

Cinnamon-Spiced Sweet Potatoes

Prep time: 5 minutes | Cook time: 3 to 4 hours | Serves 8

1 (40-ounce / 1.1-kg) can
unsweetened sweet potato
chunks, drained
1 (21-ounce / 595-g) can
lite apple pie filling

⅓ cup brown sugar
⅓ cup red hots
1 teaspoon ground
cinnamon
Nonfat cooking spray

1. Combine all ingredients in a large bowl. Pour into crock pot sprayed with nonfat cooking spray. 2. Cover. Cook on low 3 to 4 hours.

Green Bean Casserole

Prep time: 10 minutes | Cook time: 3 to 10 hours | Serves 9 to 11

3 (10-ounce / 283-g)
packages frozen, cut green
beans
2 (10½-ounce / 298-g) cans
Cheddar cheese soup
½ cup water
¼ cup chopped green
onions

1 (4-ounce / 113-g) can
sliced mushrooms, drained
1 (8-ounce / 227-g) can
water chestnuts, drained
and sliced (optional)
½ cup slivered almonds
1 teaspoon salt
¼ teaspoon pepper

1. Place all the ingredients in a lightly greased slow cooker and mix them together thoroughly. 2. Cover the cooker and cook on low for 8 to 10 hours, or on high for 3 to 4 hours, until everything is tender and well-cooked.

Garlic-Orange Mashed Sweet Potatoes

Prep time: 20 minutes | Cook time: 8 hours | Serves 1 cup

Nonstick cooking spray
4 large sweet potatoes,
peeled and cubed
1 onion, chopped
6 garlic cloves, peeled
½ cup orange juice
2 tablespoons honey

1 teaspoon salt
⅛ teaspoon freshly ground
black pepper
⅓ cup butter, at room
temperature
½ cup heavy cream

1. Spray the crock pot with the nonstick cooking spray. 2. In the crock pot , combine the sweet potatoes, onion, and garlic. 3. Pour the orange juice and honey over everything, and stir. Sprinkle with the salt and pepper. 4. Cover and cook on low for 8 hours, or until the potatoes are tender. 5. Add the butter and cream, mash using a potato masher or immersion blender, and serve.

Potato Filling

Prep time: 40 minutes | Cook time: 3 hours | Serves 20

1 cup celery, chopped fine
1 medium onion, minced
½ cup butter
2 (15-ounce / 425-g)
packages low-fat bread
cubes
6 eggs, beaten

1 quart fat-free milk
1 quart mashed potatoes
3 teaspoons salt
2 pinches saffron
1 cup boiling water
1 teaspoon black pepper

1. In a skillet, sauté the celery and onion in butter until softened and translucent. 2. Combine the sautéed vegetables with the bread cubes in a large bowl. Stir in the remaining ingredients and add more milk if the mixture feels too dry. 3. Transfer the mixture into one large or several medium-sized slow cookers. Cook on high for 3 hours, stirring occasionally from the bottom to ensure the filling doesn't stick.

Crocked Scalloped Potatoes

Prep time: 20 minutes | Cook time: 7 hours | Serves ¾ cup

Nonstick cooking spray
3 large russet potatoes,
peeled and thinly sliced
1 onion, finely chopped
3 garlic cloves, minced
1 teaspoon dried basil
leaves
1 teaspoon salt
⅛ teaspoon freshly ground
black pepper

1 cup grated Havarti
cheese
½ cup grated white
Cheddar cheese
½ cup light cream
½ cup heavy cream
2 tablespoons butter
⅓ cup grated Parmesan
cheese

1. Spray the crock pot with the nonstick cooking spray. 2. In the crock pot , layer the potatoes, onion, garlic, basil, salt, pepper, Havarti cheese, and Cheddar cheese, making about 4 layers. 3. In a small saucepan over high heat, heat the light cream, heavy cream, and butter until the butter melts, about a minute. Pour the mixture into the crock pot , and sprinkle with the Parmesan cheese. 4. Cover and cook on low for 7 hours, or until the potatoes are tender, and serve.

Apple and Squash Mélange

Prep time: 25 minutes | Cook time: 6 to 8 hours | Serves 6

1 large butternut squash, peeled, seeded, and cut into ¼-inch slices

2 medium cooking apples, cored and cut into ¼-inch slices

3 tablespoons raisins (optional)

3 tablespoons reduced-calorie pancake syrup

¼ cup apple cider or apple juice

1. Layer half of the following ingredients in crock pot : squash, apples, and raisins. 2. Drizzle with half the syrup. 3. Repeat layers. 4. Pour cider over the top. 5. Cook on low 6 to 8 hours, or until squash is tender.

Pakistani Sweet Rice with Cardamom

Prep time: 10 minutes | Cook time: 2¼ hours | Serves 6 to 8

2 cups basmati rice
4 tablespoons butter or ghee
4 cups hot water
1 large pinch saffron, crushed and mixed with 2 tablespoons hot water, or a

yellow food coloring
6 green cardamom pods
¾ to 1 cup sugar
2 tablespoons crushed unsalted pistachios
2 tablespoons slivered almonds

1. Wash the rice in a few changes of water until it runs clear, and then soak it in warm water for 10 minutes. 2. Rub a little of the butter or ghee on the inside of your crock pot and turn it to high. Drain the washed rice and place it in the crock pot . Add the hot water and saffron water (or the food coloring). Stir to mix. This should color the rice, giving it the bright yellow it's famous for. 3. Cover and cook for 2 hours on high. Stir the rice halfway through the cooking time. When cooked, remove the rice and set it aside in a colander. 4. Turn the cooker to high and add the rest of the butter to melt, then crack in the cardamom pods. Stir in the sugar and 4 tablespoons of water (add a little more if required). Stir to melt the sugar. 5. Cook gently for about 5 minutes to produce a syrup. Add most of the nuts, reserving some for a garnish. 6. Gently stir the rice back into the cooker and fold it, so that each grain is coated with the sugar syrup. 7. Cover and turn the cooker to low. Cook for another 5 to 10 minutes. 8. Serve warm, topped with the remaining nuts.

Chocolate Pot De Crème

Prep time: 10 minutes | Cook time: 3 hours | Serves 6

6 egg yolks
2 cups heavy (whipping) cream
⅓ cup cocoa powder
1 tablespoon pure vanilla extract

½ teaspoon liquid stevia
Whipped coconut cream, for garnish (optional)
Shaved dark chocolate, for garnish (optional)

1. In a mixing bowl, beat together the egg yolks, heavy cream, cocoa powder, vanilla extract, and stevia until the mixture is smooth and fully combined. 2. Pour the mixture into a 1½-quart baking dish and carefully set the dish inside the slow cooker insert. 3. Add enough hot water to the slow cooker to create a water bath that comes halfway up the sides of the baking dish. 4. Cover the slow cooker and let it cook

on low for 3 hours, allowing the custard to thicken and set. 5. Once cooking is complete, carefully remove the dish from the slow cooker and allow it to cool to room temperature. 6. Transfer the cooled dessert to the refrigerator and chill for several hours before serving, optionally garnished with whipped coconut cream and shaved dark chocolate.

Brownie Chocolate Cake

Prep time: 10 minutes | Cook time: 3 hours | Serves 12

½ cup plus 1 tablespoon unsalted butter, melted, divided
1½ cups almond flour
¾ cup cocoa powder
¾ cup granulated erythritol
1 teaspoon baking powder

¼ teaspoon fine salt
1 cup heavy (whipping) cream
3 eggs, beaten
2 teaspoons pure vanilla extract
1 cup whipped cream

1. Coat the insert of the slow cooker with 1 tablespoon of melted butter to prevent sticking. 2. In a large bowl, combine the almond flour, cocoa powder, erythritol, baking powder, and salt, stirring well to ensure everything is evenly mixed. 3. In a separate bowl, whisk together the remaining ½ cup of melted butter, heavy cream, eggs, and vanilla extract until the mixture is smooth and well incorporated. 4. Add the wet ingredients to the dry ingredients, stirring until fully combined, and then spoon the batter into the prepared slow cooker insert. 5. Cover and cook on low for 3 hours, then carefully remove the insert from the slow cooker and let the cake sit for 1 hour to set. 6. Serve the cake warm, topped with a dollop of whipped cream.

Cinnamon Raisin Rice Pudding

Prep time: 5 minutes | Cook time: 6 to 7 hours | Serves 4 to 6

½ cup white rice, uncooked
½ cup sugar
1 teaspoon vanilla
1 teaspoon lemon extract
1 cup plus 2 tablespoons milk

1 teaspoon butter
2 eggs, beaten
1 teaspoon cinnamon
½ cup raisins
1 cup whipping cream
Whipped nutmeg

1. Combine all ingredients except whipped cream and nutmeg in crock pot . Stir well. 2. Cover pot. Cook on low 6 to 7 hours, until rice is tender and milk absorbed. Be sure to stir once every 2 hours during cooking. 3. Pour into bowl. Cover with plastic wrap and chill several hours. 4. Before serving, fold in whipped cream and sprinkle with nutmeg.

Blood Orange Upside-Down Cake

Prep time: 25 minutes | Cook time: 4 hours | Serves 6 to 8

Orange Layer:
5 tablespoons unsalted butter, cut into small pieces, plus more for crock pot crock
¾ cup firmly packed dark brown sugar
3 tablespoons dark rum
2 pounds (907 g) blood oranges (about 6), sliced, peeled, with all of the bitter white pith removed
½ teaspoon ground cardamom
Cake:
¾ cups cake flour
¾ teaspoons baking powder
½ teaspoon ground cinnamon
¼ teaspoon ground nutmeg
¼ teaspoon salt
4 tablespoons unsalted butter, at room temperature
⅔ cup granulated sugar
1 egg, at room temperature
1 egg yolk, at room temperature
2 tablespoons whole milk, at room temperature
2 cups vanilla ice cream, for serving (optional)

Make the Orange Layer: 1. Grease the inside of the slow cooker insert, line it with foil, then butter the foil generously. 2. Sprinkle the melted butter, brown sugar, and rum over the foil in the bottom of the crock pot. Arrange the orange slices in a slightly overlapping pattern over the sugar mixture, then sprinkle with cardamom. Press the orange slices gently into the sugar.

Make the Cake: 3. In a large bowl, sift together the flour, baking powder, cinnamon, nutmeg, and salt. Whisk to combine evenly. 4. In a separate bowl, use an electric mixer on low speed to beat the butter and sugar together until just blended. Increase the speed to high and continue beating for about 10 minutes, until light and fluffy, occasionally scraping down the sides of the bowl. 5. Beat in the egg and egg yolk, one at a time, allowing each to fully incorporate before adding the next. 6. Gradually add the flour mixture to the butter-sugar mixture in three parts, alternating with the milk in two parts. Start and end with the flour, mixing briefly on medium speed to form a smooth batter. 7. Pour the batter over the prepared orange layer in the crock pot, spreading it evenly with a spatula. 8. Place a doubled length of paper towel over the top of the crock pot insert, tucking it under the lid to create a tight seal. 9. Cover and cook on high for about 3½ hours, or until the cake edges are slightly browned and the center springs back when touched. Turn off the slow cooker and let the cake set, uncovered, for 20 minutes. 10. Using the foil, lift the cake out of the crock pot and place it on the counter to cool for another 30 minutes. Remove the foil and carefully invert the cake onto a platter, so the caramelized oranges are on top. 11. Slice or spoon the cake into bowls and serve with a scoop of ice cream, if desired.

Cinnamon Apple Crumble

Prep time: 10 minutes | Cook time: 2 to 3 hours | Serves 6 to 8

1 quart canned apple pie filling
¾ cup quick oatmeal
½ cup brown sugar
½ cup flour
¼ cup butter, at room temperature

1. Place pie filling in crock pot . 2. Combine remaining ingredients until crumbly. Sprinkle over apple filling. 3. Cover. Cook on low 2 to 3 hours.

Raspberry Peach Bread Pudding

Prep time: 20 minutes | Cook time: 3 hours | Serves 6 to 8

2 (16-ounce / 454-g) bags frozen unsweetened raspberries, defrosted and drained
1 cup superfine sugar
2 teaspoons fresh lemon juice
8 cups torn stale egg bread, challah, or croissants
12 medium peaches, peeled, pitted, and coarsely chopped, or 3 (16-ounce / 454-g) packages frozen peaches, defrosted, drained, and coarsely chopped
3 cups heavy cream
8 large eggs
Grated zest of 1 orange
¼ cup Grand Marnier or other orange-flavored liqueur or 1 teaspoon orange extract
1½ cups granulated sugar

1. Coat the insert of a 5- to 7-quart crock pot with nonstick cooking spray or line it with a slow-cooker liner according to the manufacturer's directions. 2. Heat the berries, superfine sugar, and lemon juice in a small saucepan until the mixture comes to a boil. Taste the syrup and add more sugar is it is too tart. Strain the mixture through a fine-mesh; you should have ⅔ to ¾ cup of syrup. Put the bread in the slow-cooker insert and stir in the peaches. Pour the raspberry syrup over all. 3. Whisk together the cream, eggs, orange zest, Grand Marnier, and granulated sugar in a large mixing bowl until blended. Pour over the bread in the slow-cooker insert and push the bread down to submerge it. 4. Cover and cook on high for about 3 hours, until puffed and an instant-read meat thermometer inserted in the center registers 185ºF (85ºC). Uncover and allow to cool for 30 minutes. 5. Serve from the cooker set on warm.

Scandinavian Fruit Soup

Prep time: 5 minutes | Cook time: 8 hours | Serves 12

1 cup dried apricots

1 cup dried sliced apples

1 cup dried pitted prunes

1 cup canned pitted red cherries

½ cup quick-cooking tapioca

1 cup grape juice or red

wine

3 cups water, or more

½ cup orange juice

¼ cup lemon juice

1 tablespoon grated orange peel

½ cup brown sugar

1. In the slow cooker, combine apricots, apples, prunes, cherries, tapioca, and grape juice. Add enough water to cover the fruit mixture. 2. Cover and cook on low for a minimum of 8 hours, allowing the fruit to soften and the flavors to meld. 3. About 10 minutes before serving, stir in the remaining ingredients. 4. Serve the dish warm or chilled, depending on your preference.

Chocolate Almond Rice Pudding

Prep time: 10 minutes | Cook time: 2½ to 3½ hours | Serves 4

4 cups white rice, cooked

¾ cup sugar

¼ cup baking cocoa powder

3 tablespoons butter, melted

1 teaspoon vanilla

2 (12-ounce / 340-g) cans evaporated milk

Whipped cream

Sliced toasted almonds

Maraschino cherries

1. Combine first 6 ingredients in greased crock pot . 2. Cover. Cook on low 2½ to 3½ hours, or until liquid is absorbed. 3. Serve warm or chilled. Top individual servings with a dollop of whipped cream, sliced toasted almonds, and a maraschino cherry.

Rum Raisin Rice Pudding

Prep time: 10 minutes | Cook time: 4 hours | Serves 6

½ cup raisins

¼ cup dark rum

1 (12-ounce / 340-g) can evaporated milk

1½ cups water

⅓ cup granulated sugar

¾ cup Arborio rice

¼ teaspoon salt

¼ teaspoon ground nutmeg

1. Combine the raisins and rum in a small bowl. Cover and

set aside. 2. Combine the evaporated milk and 1½ cups water in a heavy medium saucepan. Bring to a simmer over medium heat. Add the sugar, stirring to dissolve. Remove from the heat. 3. Pour the milk mixture into the crock pot . Stir in the rice and salt. 4. Cover and cook on low for 4 hours, stirring after 1 hour and again after 3 hours. The pudding is finished when it is just set in the center. 5. Drain the raisins, and stir them into the pudding. Stir in the nutmeg. Let stand, uncovered, 10 minutes. Serve warm, or chill in the fridge for about 3 hours in dessert cups.

Honeyed Cherry Apples

Prep time: 15 minutes | Cook time: 4 hours | Serves 2

3 apples

1 tablespoon freshly squeezed lemon juice

⅓ cup dried cherries

2 tablespoons apple cider

2 tablespoons honey

¼ cup water

1. Cut about half an inch off the top of each of the apples, and peel a small strip of the skin away around the top. 2. Using a small serrated spoon or melon baller, core the apples, making sure not to go through the bottom. Drizzle with the lemon juice. 3. Fill the apples with the dried cherries. Carefully spoon the cider and honey into the apples. 4. Place the apples in the crock pot . Pour the water around the apples. 5. Cover and cook on low for 4 hours, or until the apples are soft, and serve.

Creamy Rice Pudding

Prep time: 10 minutes | Cook time: 3 hours | Serves 6 to 8

1 teaspoon butter or ghee

½ cup basmati rice, washed and drained

2 tablespoons sugar

½ teaspoon green cardamom seeds, lightly crushed

2 green cardamom pods

2 tablespoons golden raisins (optional)

5 cups whole milk

2 tablespoons crushed unsalted pistachios

1. Grease the bottom and sides of the slow cooker insert with butter or ghee. 2. Add the rice, sugar, cardamom seeds, cardamom pods, raisins, and milk to the crock pot, stirring to combine. 3. Cover and cook on high for 3 hours, stirring once or twice throughout the cooking time. 4. This dish can be served either hot or cold. It will thicken as it cools. Before serving, top with chopped nuts for added crunch and flavor.

Peanut Butter Crunch Clusters

Prep time: 15 minutes | Cook time: 1 hour | Makes 6½ dozen

2 pounds (907 g) white candy coating, coarsely chopped	4 cups Cap'n Crunch cereal
1½ cups peanut butter	4 cups crisp rice cereal
½ teaspoon almond extract (optional)	4 cups miniature marshmallows

1. Place candy coating in a 5-quart crock pot . Cover and cook on high for 1 hour. Add peanut butter. Stir in extract if desired. 2. In a large bowl, combine the cereals and marshmallows. Stir in the peanut butter mixture until well coated. Drop by tablespoonfuls onto waxed paper. Let stand until set. Store at room temperature.

Butterscotch Bread Pudding with Brown-Butter Rum Sauce

Prep time: 25 minutes | Cook time: 3 hours | Serves 8

Nonstick cooking spray	8 cups lightly packed 1-inch cubes of day-old brioche
Bread Pudding:	
4 large eggs, plus 1 egg yolk	¾ cup butterscotch chips
¾ cup sugar	¾ cup chopped pecans
1½ cups milk, room temperature	Brown-Butter Rum Sauce:
2 cups heavy cream, room temperature	½ cup packed dark brown sugar
2 tablespoons unsalted butter, melted and cooled	4 tablespoons unsalted butter
2 teaspoon vanilla extract	⅓ cup whipping cream
Pinch coarse salt	¼ cup dark rum

1. Begin by lightly greasing the insert of a 7-quart slow cooker with cooking spray and preheating the cooker. For the bread pudding, 2. In a large mixing bowl, whisk together the eggs, egg yolk, and sugar until fully combined. Stir in the milk, cream, melted butter, vanilla extract, and a pinch of salt. 3. Add the bread cubes, butterscotch chips, and chopped pecans to the slow cooker, stirring to mix everything together. Pour the egg mixture evenly over the bread, making sure it's well-soaked. Cover the slow cooker and cook on low for about 3 hours, or on high for 1½ hours, until a knife inserted in the center comes out clean. 4. Remove the lid and continue cooking on low for an additional 30 minutes, or on high for about 15 minutes, until a light crust forms on top. Let the bread pudding sit uncovered for at least 15 minutes before serving. For the sauce, 5. In a saucepan, combine the brown sugar, butter, cream, and rum. Bring the mixture to a boil over medium heat, stirring constantly. Let it boil for 3 to 4 minutes, continuing to stir, until the sauce slightly thickens. Drizzle the warm sauce over each serving of the bread pudding.

Cinnamon Apple Pear Crumble

Prep time: 20 minutes | Cook time: 7 hours | Serves 2

Nonstick cooking spray	2 tablespoons butter, plus 3 tablespoons cut into cubes, divided
4 apples, peeled and sliced	
2 pears, peeled and sliced	
¼ cup brown sugar	½ cup light cream
1 tablespoon freshly squeezed lemon juice	1 cup all-purpose flour
½ teaspoon ground cinnamon	½ cup rolled oats
	½ cup chopped pecans
	⅓ cup granulated sugar

1. Spray the crock pot with the nonstick cooking spray. 2. In the crock pot , combine the apple and pear slices; sprinkle with the brown sugar, lemon juice, and cinnamon, and mix. Dot with 2 tablespoons of butter and pour the cream over everything. 3. In a medium bowl, combine the flour, oats, pecans, and granulated sugar. Add the remaining 3 tablespoons of butter cubes, and cut in with two knives or a pastry blender until crumbly. Sprinkle the mixture over the fruit. 4. Cover and cook on low for 7 hours, or until the fruit is tender.

Apple Appeal

Prep time: 10 minutes | Cook time: 4 to 5 hours | Serves 6

6 baking apples, peeled, cored, and quartered	¾ teaspoon Asian five-spice powder
¼ teaspoon nutmeg	¼ cup apple juice
2 tablespoons sugar	

1. Add the prepared apples to the slow cooker insert. 2. In a small bowl, combine all the remaining ingredients and mix well. 3. Pour the mixture over the apples in the slow cooker, stirring gently to ensure the apples are coated. 4. Cover and cook on low for 4 to 5 hours, or until the apples reach your desired level of tenderness. 5. Serve the apples either sliced or mashed, and enjoy them warm, cold, or at room temperature.

Tiramisu Bread Pudding

Prep time: 15 minutes | Cook time: 3 hours | Serves 10

½ cup water
⅓ cup granulated sugar
1½ tablespoons instant espresso granules
2 tablespoons coffee-flavored liqueur (like Kahlúa)
2 cups whole milk
2 large eggs, lightly beaten

8 ounces (227 g) French bread, cut into 1-inch cubes (about 8 cups)
Nonstick cooking oil spray
⅓ cup Mascarpone cheese
1 teaspoon vanilla extract
2 teaspoons unsweetened cocoa powder

1. In a small saucepan, combine the water, sugar, and espresso granules. Heat over medium-high until it comes to a boil, then let it boil for 1 minute, stirring occasionally. Remove from heat and stir in the liqueur. 2. In a large bowl, whisk together 1¾ cups of milk and the eggs. Gradually whisk in the espresso mixture, then fold in the bread cubes, making sure they are well coated. 3. Spray a 2½-quart round baking dish with nonstick cooking spray. Pour the bread mixture into the dish and place it in the slow cooker. Cover and cook on low for about 2 hours, or until the pudding is set. Once done, remove the dish from the slow cooker and allow it to cool. Refrigerate the pudding for at least 3 hours to chill. 4. In a small bowl, whisk together the remaining ¼ cup of milk, mascarpone cheese, and vanilla until smooth. To serve, spoon the chilled bread pudding onto plates, topping each portion with the mascarpone sauce and a light dusting of cocoa powder.

Stewed Apricots

Prep time: 10 minutes | Cook time: 2 to 4 hours | Serves 6 to 8

1⅓ pounds (605 g) dried apricots, pitted
1 teaspoon ground cinnamon
1 cup granulated sugar

1 to 1¼ cups water
⅓ cup heavy cream
2 tablespoons toasted almond slivers

1. Set the slow cooker to high and place the apricots, cinnamon, sugar, and water into the pot. 2. Cover and cook on high for 2 hours, or on low for 4 hours, until the apricots are tender and the flavors have melded together. 3. Transfer the mixture to a large bowl and allow it to cool before placing it in the refrigerator to chill. 4. Just before serving, whip the cream until stiff peaks form. Spoon the chilled apricot mixture into individual glasses, then top with freshly whipped cream and a sprinkle of nuts.

Piña Colada Bread Pudding

Prep time: 15 minutes | Cook time: 3 hours | Serves 6 to 8

8 cups torn stale Hawaiian sweet egg bread, challah, or croissants
2 cups ½-inch chunks fresh pineapple
1 cup chopped macadamia nuts
1½ cups shredded

sweetened coconut
3 cups heavy cream
8 large eggs
1 tablespoon vanilla extract or bean paste
¼ cup dark rum
1½ cups sugar

1. Lightly grease the insert of a 5- to 7-quart slow cooker with nonstick cooking spray, or line it with a slow-cooker liner as directed by the manufacturer. 2. Place the bread into the slow cooker insert, then add the pineapple, nuts, and coconut. Toss everything together to combine. In a large bowl, whisk the cream, eggs, vanilla, rum, and sugar until smooth. Pour this mixture over the bread and gently press the bread down to ensure it's fully submerged. 3. Cover and cook on high for about 3 hours, until the pudding is puffed and an instant-read thermometer inserted into the center reads 185°F (85°C). Once done, uncover and let it cool for 30 minutes. 4. Serve directly from the slow cooker, set to warm, for easy enjoyment.

Reamy Arborio Rice Pudding

Prep time: 10 minutes | Cook time: 2½ to 3 hours | Serves 6 to 8

5 cups whole milk
2 cups heavy cream
1¼ cups sugar
1 teaspoon vanilla bean paste
½ teaspoon freshly grated

nutmeg
1 cup Arborio or other medium-grain rice, rinsed several times with cold water and drained

1. Coat the insert of a 5- to 7-quart crock pot with nonstick cooking spr ay. Whisk together the milk, cream, sugar, vanilla bean paste, and nutmeg in a large bowl and pour into the slow-cooker insert. Add the rice and stir to combine. 2. Cover and cook on low for 2½ to 3 hours, until the pudding is soft and creamy and the rice is tender. Remove the cover, turn off the cooker, and allow to cool for 30 minutes. 3. Serve warm, at room temperature, or chilled.

Peanut Butter and Hot Fudge Pudding Cake

Prep time: 10 minutes | Cook time: 2 to 3 hours | Serves 6

½ cup flour
¼ cup sugar
¾ teaspoon baking powder
⅓ cup milk
1 tablespoon oil
½ teaspoon vanilla

¼ cup peanut butter
½ cup sugar
3 tablespoons unsweetened cocoa powder
1 cup boiling water
Vanilla ice cream

1. In a bowl, mix together the flour, ¼ cup sugar, and baking powder. Add the milk, oil, and vanilla extract, stirring until smooth. Incorporate the peanut butter into the mixture, then pour it into the slow cooker insert. 2. In a separate bowl, combine the remaining ½ cup sugar with the cocoa powder. 3. Gradually add the boiling water, stirring until the cocoa mixture is smooth. Pour this over the batter in the slow cooker, but do not stir. 4. Cover and cook on high for 2 to 3 hours, or until a toothpick inserted into the center comes out clean. Serve warm, topped with a scoop of ice cream for a delicious treat.

Slow-Cooked Vanilla Cheesecake

Prep time: 25 minutes | Cook time: 2 hours | Serves 6

Nonstick cooking spray
Crust:
¾ cup graham cracker crumbs
2 tablespoons unsalted butter, melted
2 tablespoons sugar
Filling:
16 ounces (454 g) cream

cheese, softened
½ cup sugar
2 tablespoons all-purpose flour
2 teaspoon vanilla extract
2 large eggs, room temperature
½ cup plain yogurt or sour cream

1. Lightly coat a 6-inch springform pan with cooking spray; line bottom with parchment and lightly spray. Fill a 5- to 6-quart crock pot with ½ inch hot water. Set three 1-inch balls of foil in center of crock pot . Wrap slow-cooker lid tightly with a clean kitchen towel, gathering ends at top (to absorb condensation). Make the Crust: 2. Combine crumbs, butter, and sugar. Press mixture evenly on bottom and about 1 inch up sides of springform pan. Make the Filling: 3. In a food processor, pulse cream cheese, sugar, flour, and vanilla until smooth. Add eggs and process until combined. Add yogurt and process until smooth, scraping down sides of bowl. Pour filling into pan. Gently tap pan on work surface to remove air bubbles. 4. Set pan on aluminum balls in

crock pot . Cover and cook on high until set and an instant-read thermometer inserted in center registers 155ºF (68ºC), 1½ to 2 hours (do not cook on low). Turn off crock pot and let cake rest, covered, 1 hour. 5. Carefully transfer pan to a wire rack to cool completely, then refrigerate until chilled, at least 4 hours and preferably overnight. Carefully remove outer ring from pan and transfer cake to a plate (remove parchment). Use a warm knife to cut into wedges, wiping blade after each cut.

Spiced Apples

Prep time: 5 minutes | Cook time: 4 to 5 hours | Serves 10 to 12

16 cups sliced apples, peeled or unpeeled, divided
½ cup brown sugar, divided

3 tablespoons minute tapioca, divided
1 teaspoon ground cinnamon, divided

1. Begin by layering half of the sliced apples in the slow cooker, followed by sugar, tapioca, and cinnamon. 2. Create a second layer with the remaining apples, sugar, tapioca, and cinnamon. 3. Cover the slow cooker and cook on high for 4 hours, or on low for 5 hours, until the apples are tender. 4. Stir the mixture before serving to ensure everything is well combined.

Spiced Fruit Compote

Prep time: 30 minutes | Cook time: 3 to 8 hours | Serves 10 to 12

3 medium-size pears, peeled, cored, and cubed
1 (16-ounce / 454-g) can pineapple, in cubes or chunks, with the juice
1 cup quartered dried apricots
3 tablespoons frozen orange juice concentrate
2 tablespoons packed light brown sugar

1 tablespoon quick-cooking tapioca
1 teaspoon grated peeled fresh ginger (or ½ teaspoon dried ground ginger)
2 cups pitted dark, sweet cherries
1 cup toasted shredded unsweetened coconut
1 cup chopped and toasted macadamia nuts or pecans

1. In the slow cooker, combine the pears, pineapple with its juice, apricots, orange juice concentrate, brown sugar, tapioca, and ginger, stirring to blend everything together. 2. Cover and cook on low for 6 to 8 hours, or on high for 3 to 4 hours. About 30 minutes before the cooking time ends, stir in the cherries. 3. Serve warm, topped with coconut and chopped nuts for added texture and flavor.

Caramelized Banana Bread Pudding

Prep time: 15 minutes | Cook time: 3 hours | Serves 8

½ cup (1 stick) unsalted butter

2 cups firmly packed light brown sugar

4 medium bananas, cut into ½-inch rounds

8 large eggs

3 cups heavy cream

¼ cup dark rum

1 teaspoon ground cinnamon

1 tablespoon vanilla extract or vanilla bean paste

8 cups 1-inch cubes stale challah, egg bread, or Hawaiian sweet egg bread

¼ cup cinnamon sugar

Whipped cream for serving

1. Coat the insert of a 5- to 7-quart crock pot with nonstick cooking spray or line the insert with a slow-cooker liner according to the manufacturer's directions. 2. Melt the butter in a large skillet over medium-high heat. Add 1 cup of the sugar and heat, stirring, until the sugar melts. Add the bananas and stir to coat. Remove the skillet from the heat and allow the bananas to cool slightly. 3. Whisk together the eggs, cream, remaining 1 cup sugar, rum, cinnamon, and vanilla in a large bowl. Add the bread to the custard and stir to blend, making sure to saturate the bread. Spoon half of the custard-soaked bread into the cooker and top with half the bananas. Repeat the layers, ending with the bananas. 4. Sprinkle the top with the cinnamon sugar. Cover and cook on high for about 3 hours, until puffed and an instant-read thermometer registers 185ºF (85ºC). Allow the pudding to cool for about 30 minutes. 5. Serve with whipped cream.

Espresso Chocolate Bread Pudding

Prep time: 15 minutes | Cook time: 3 hours | Serves 8

8 cups torn stale egg bread, challah or croissants

2 cups chocolate chips or chopped chocolate

3 cups heavy cream

1 cup brewed espresso or strong coffee

8 large eggs

1 tablespoon vanilla extract

2 teaspoons ground cinnamon

1½ cups sugar

½ cup sugar mixed with 1 teaspoon ground cinnamon, for garnish (optional)

Hot fudge sauce for drizzling (optional)

1. Spray the insert of a 5- to 7-quart crock pot with nonstick cooking spray or line it with a slow-cooker liner according to the manufacturer's directions. 2. Spread the torn bread evenly in the bottom of the slow-cooker insert and sprinkle with the chocolate chips. Whisk together the cream, espresso, eggs, vanilla, cinnamon, and sugar in a large bowl until blended. Pour over the bread and chocolate, pushing the bread down to submerge it. 3. Sprinkle the pudding with the cinnamon sugar (if using). Cover the crock pot and cook on high for about 3 hours, until puffed and an instant-read thermometer inserted in the center registers 185ºF (85ºC). Uncover and allow the pudding to cool for about 30 minutes. 4. Serve from the cooker set on warm and accompany with hot fudge sauce for drizzling.

Cherries Jubilee Lava Cake

Prep time: 20 minutes | Cook time: 2 hours | Serves 4 to 6

Cherries:

2 (16-ounce / 454-g) bags frozen unsweetened pitted sweet cherries, defrosted and drained

¼ cup sugar

2 tablespoons cornstarch

2 tablespoons brandy or Grand Marnier

Chocolate Cake:

½ cup milk

3 tablespoons unsalted

butter, melted

1 teaspoon vanilla bean paste

1 cup granulated sugar

1 cup all-purpose flour

½ cup cocoa powder (make sure to use natural cocoa powder, not Dutch process)

2 teaspoons baking powder

¾ cup firmly packed light brown sugar

1¼ cups boiling water

1. Lightly grease the insert of a 3½- to 4-quart slow cooker with nonstick cooking spray. Add all the cherries, sugar, cornstarch, and brandy, stirring well to combine. 2. In a separate bowl, mix together the milk, butter, and vanilla bean paste. Gradually incorporate the granulated sugar, flour, ¼ cup of cocoa powder, and baking powder, stirring until smooth. 3. Carefully spread the batter evenly over the cherries in the slow cooker insert. In a small bowl, mix the brown sugar and the remaining ¼ cup of cocoa powder, then sprinkle it evenly over the batter. Pour the boiling water over the top (do not stir). 4. Cover and cook on high for 2 hours, or until a skewer inserted into the center comes out clean. Once done, uncover and let the dessert cool for about 20 minutes. 5. Serve directly from the slow cooker, ensuring the cherries remain hidden beneath the cake, creating a delightful surprise when spooned out.

Double Chocolate Croissant Bread Pudding

Prep time: 15 minutes | Cook time: 3 hours | Serves 6 to 8

8 cups torn stale croissants, egg bread, or challah
3 cups chopped bittersweet or semisweet chocolate
4 tablespoons (½ stick) unsalted butter, melted
3 cups heavy cream

8 large eggs
1 tablespoon vanilla bean paste or extract
1 cup sugar

1. Lightly grease the insert of a 5- to 7-quart slow cooker with nonstick cooking spray, or line it with a slow-cooker liner as per the manufacturer's instructions. 2. Arrange the bread slices in the slow cooker and sprinkle with 1½ cups of the chocolate chips. In a small saucepan, melt the remaining chocolate with the butter over low heat, then remove from heat and let it cool. 3. In a large mixing bowl, whisk together the melted chocolate, cream, eggs, vanilla bean paste, and sugar until well combined, though the mixture may appear slightly curdled. Pour the mixture over the bread and chocolate, pressing the bread down gently to ensure it's fully submerged. 4. Cover and cook on high for about 3 hours, until the pudding is puffed and an instant-read thermometer inserted into the center reads 185°F (85°C). Once cooked, uncover and let it cool for 30 minutes. 5. Serve directly from the slow cooker, keeping it on the warm setting.

Peanut Butter Fudge Cake

Prep time: 10 minutes | Cook time: 2 to 2½ hours | Serves 8 to 10

2 cups dry milk chocolate cake mix
½ cup water
6 tablespoons peanut butter

2 eggs
½ cup chopped nuts

1. Combine all ingredients in electric mixer bowl. Beat for 2 minutes. 2. Spray interior of a baking insert, designed to fit into your crock pot . Flour interior of greased insert. Pour batter into insert. Place insert in crock pot . 3. Cover insert with 8 paper towels. 4. Cover cooker. Cook on high 2 to 2½ hours, or until toothpick inserted into center of cake comes out clean. 5. Allow cake to cool. Then invert onto a serving plate, cut, and serve.

Jalapeño Cranberry Relish

Prep time: 5 minutes | Cook time: 2 to 3 hours | Serves 8

1 (16-ounce / 454-g) can whole berry cranberry sauce
1 (10½-ounce / 298-g) jar jalapeño jelly

2 tablespoons chopped fresh cilantro

1. Combine ingredients in crock pot . 2. Cover. Cook on low 2 to 3 hours. 3. Cool. Serve at room temperature.

Appendix 1

Measurement Conversion Char

VOLUME EQUIVALENTS(DRY)

US STANDARD	METRIC (APPROXIMATE)
1/8 teaspoon	0.5 mL
1/4 teaspoon	1 mL
1/2 teaspoon	2 mL
3/4 teaspoon	4 mL
1 teaspoon	5 mL
1 tablespoon	15 mL
1/4 cup	59 mL
1/2 cup	118 mL
3/4 cup	177 mL
1 cup	235 mL
2 cups	475 mL
3 cups	700 mL
4 cups	1 L

WEIGHT EQUIVALENTS

US STANDARD	METRIC (APPROXIMATE)
1 ounce	28 g
2 ounces	57 g
5 ounces	142 g
10 ounces	284 g
15 ounces	425 g
16 ounces (1 pound)	455 g
1.5 pounds	680 g
2 pounds	907 g

VOLUME EQUIVALENTS(LIQUID)

US STANDARD	US STANDARD (OUNCES)	METRIC (APPROXIMATE)
2 tablespoons	1 fl.oz.	30 mL
1/4 cup	2 fl.oz.	60 mL
1/2 cup	4 fl.oz.	120 mL
1 cup	8 fl.oz.	240 mL
1 1/2 cup	12 fl.oz.	355 mL
2 cups or 1 pint	16 fl.oz.	475 mL
4 cups or 1 quart	32 fl.oz.	1 L
1 gallon	128 fl.oz.	4 L

TEMPERATURES EQUIVALENTS

FAHRENHEIT(F)	CELSIUS(C) (APPROXIMATE)
225 °F	107 °C
250 °F	120 °C
275 °F	135 °C
300 °F	150 °C
325 °F	160 °C
350 °F	180 °C
375 °F	190 °C
400 °F	205 °C
425 °F	220 °C
450 °F	235 °C
475 °F	245 °C
500 °F	260 °C

Appendix 2

Index

Made in the USA
Las Vegas, NV
02 January 2025

15659480R00057